BE#1

"THANK GOD IT'S MONDAY!"

1001 WAYS

...werment 〜 Self-Directed Teams

TO ENERGIZE

Continuous Improvement

EMPLOYEES

Inspiring Personal Initiative & Risk

BY BOB NELSON

Author of the bestselling *1001 Ways to Reward Employees*

UPC

0 19628 10160 0

"We all know the power of a good story. A good example provides us with much the same. In *1001 Ways to Energize Employees,* Bob Nelson has given us a resource that not only shows us what others have done to get the best from employees, but what we can do as well."

JACK CANFIELD, PRESIDENT,
SELF-ESTEEM SEMINARS CO-AUTHOR, CHICKEN SOUP FOR THE SOUL

"Energized employees are a vital force in any successful organization. Bob Nelson's new book shows us how to unleash this power through a wealth of practical examples that are sure to inspire new heights of employee performance."

J.W. MARRIOTT, JR., CHAIRMAN AND CEO,
MARRIOTT INTERNATIONAL, INC.

"Once again, Bob Nelson has cut through the smoke and mirrors, confusion, and double talk of an important area and given managers a useful tool kit. A must read."

RON ZEMKE, CO-AUTHOR,
COACHING KNOCK YOUR SOCKS OFF SERVICE

"Usually, I ignore books that claim '1001' anything. But as soon as I started reading Bob Nelson's new book, I found myself circling item after item that had great value for my work and my clients."

JOEL BARKER, PRESIDENT
INFINITY LIMITED, INC., AUTHOR, PARADIGMS

"I couldn't agree more with Nelson's findings, and his book backs them up with quick, usable ideas we should all consider."

HAL ROSENBLUTH, CEO, ROSENBLUTH INTERNATIONAL

"Nelson has provided a catalogue of practical and do-able ideas and suggestions. Start anywhere in the book, but get started in enabling others to act."

BARRY Z. POSNER, PH.D., PROFESSOR OF ORGANIZATIONAL BEHAVIOR,
LEAVEY SCHOOL OF BUSINESS AND ADMINISTRATION, SANTA CLARA UNIVERSITY

"Bob Nelson's new book is filled with practical wisdom that can help any business become more energized, more successful, and yes—more fun!"

MATT WEINSTEIN, FOUNDING PRESIDENT, PLAYFAIR, INC.
AUTHOR, MANAGING TO HAVE FUN

"This is a great book! It is a high performance handbook you can use to be a better manager in everything you do that affects other people."

BRIAN TRACY, PRESIDENT, BRIAN TRACY INTERNATIONAL,
AUTHOR, ADVANCED SELLING STRATEGIES

1001 WAYS TO ENERGIZE EMPLOYEES

BY BOB NELSON

Foreword by Jack Stack
Illustrations by Burton Morris

WORKMAN PUBLISHING · NEW YORK

Copyright ©1997 by Bob Nelson

All rights reserved. No portion of this book may be reproduced—mechanically,
electronically, or by any other means, including photocopying—without written
permission of the publisher. Published simultaneously in Canada by
Thomas Allen & Son Limited.

Library of Congress Cataloging-in-Publication Data
Nelson, Bob, 1956–
1001 ways to energize employees / by Bob Nelson.
p. cm.
Includes index.
ISBN 0-7611-0160-8
1. Employee motivation. I. Title.
HF5549.5.M63.N44 1997
658.3'14—dc21   97-10766
CIP

Cover design by Lisa Hollander
Cover and interior illustrations by Burton Morris

Workman books are available at special discount when purchased in bulk for
special premiums and sales promotions as well as for fund-raising or educational use.
Special editions or book excerpts also can be created to specification. For details,
contact the Special Sales Director at the address below.

Workman Publishing Company, Inc.
708 Broadway
New York, NY 10003-9555

Manufactured in the United States of America
First Printing May 1997
10 9

——————

Many thanks to the following for granting permission
to use excerpts from their work:

Excerpts from *Getting Employees to Fall in Love with Your Company* by Jim Harris,
Ph.D. Copyright © 1996. Reprinted by permission of the author.

Excerpts from *Eighty-Eight Assignments for Development in Place: Enhancing the
Development Challenge of Existing Jobs* by Michael M. Lombardo and Robert W.
Eichinger. Copyright © 1989. Reprinted by permission of Center for Creative Leadership,
P.O. Box 26300, Greensboro, NC. All rights reserved.

Excerpts from "Values for the '90s" by Tom Peters. Copyright © 1995. Reprinted by
permission of *Tom Peters Fast Forward*.

FOREWORD

We like things fast. We don't have time to study. The world is changing so rapidly that by the time we learn something, it has often changed in some way, shape, or form. We want information in small bites, fat-free doses that will give us a boost to a new level until the next new idea comes along. At the same time, we want satisfaction, proof that even though life is moving quickly, we are gaining on it and we are making a difference.

Well, help has finally arrived in the form of *1001 Ways to Energize Employees.* A long overdue collection of ideas from people who have done simple things to make this high-speed race a little more manageable.

Bob has spared us from new theories, models, or paradigms, instead offering us insight into most energizing techniques that managers in companies across America are successfully using today. He cuts to the heart of the matter, giving us ideas that have worked for others and will work for you if you take the time to give them a try.

Organizations need energized people. Open-book management, employee empowerment, continuous improvement, participative management, and self-directed work teams are all concepts that seek to energize employees by making them a more integral part of the workplace. Bob has researched the most practical elements of these concepts and put them into a form that makes sense and that can be put to use right away.

He allows the reader to apply a general premise to his or her own specific situation, unique needs, or constraints. He vindicates and validates the use of ideas. He gives us what will work best.

We no longer need to wait. We can get started in small, immediate ways that make a difference, confident that we will make progress if we take the initiative to act. This book confirms all those thoughts and feelings about managing people you already had in your heart and mind, and when you are through reading it you will know that you were always right.

With Bob Nelson's book, the challenge of energizing people just got a little easier.

Jack Stack, President and CEO, SRC Corporation
Author, *The Great Game of Business*

*To managers everywhere who
aren't afraid to try new ideas to get the best from
others and themselves.*

ACKNOWLEDGMENTS

It takes many to pull together a good book. First I'd like to thank the hundreds of individuals who have sent me items from their companies to use in this book. I'm also grateful to David Witt, who assisted with extensive research for the project; Michele Jansen, who helped review that research as well as hundreds of business periodicals looking for appropriate items for inclusion; and my very good friend of 27 years, Peter Economy, who played such an integral role in bringing this manuscript to fruition.

I'd also like to thank:

Ken and Margie Blanchard, cofounders of Blanchard Training and Development in San Diego, California, who have supported my efforts to publish resources to help managers.

My doctoral committee at the Claremont Graduate University—Don Gresinger, Harvey Wichman, and Joe Maciariello—for their support and for their discussions of the concepts and theories that relate to this work.

Workman Publishing and all the great people there whom I've had a chance to work with recently and over the last few years, including Peter Workman, Sally Kovalchick, Margot Herrera, Jenny Mandel, Andrea Glickson, Bert Snyder, Pat Upton, Carolan Workman, Saundra Pearson, Carbery O'Brien, Ellen Morganstern, Steve Tager, Janet Harris, Mary Kelly, Craig Hassler, Lisa Hollander, Lori S. Malkin, Annye Camara, and many others.

Other individuals who have been of great help and support to me in my professional life in recent years include my assistant, Julie Hemming; my newsletter publisher, Marilyn Harrison; my publicists, Patti Danos and Cynthia Kazan; and my agents, Margret McBride and Kenn Voegele.

Finally, I am ever so grateful for the ongoing love and support of my family—Jennifer, Daniel, Michelle, and Peggy—from whom I've stolen time to work on this project.

CONTENTS

INTRODUCTION

I n *1001 Ways to Reward Employees* I was able to show that a simple principle, well applied, could make a significant impact on the operations and success of any organization. The power of positive reinforcement and the notion that "you get what you reward" was common sense, but not common practice in most organizations I'd observed.

With *1001 Ways,* managers who were interested in improving the morale and performance of their workers suddenly had a valuable resource at their fingertips—a book full of ideas other managers had successfully used for obtaining improved performance from their employees. As an added bonus, managers could see that the least expensive and relatively easy rewards were ironically often the most motivating to employees. Any manager could put the principle of "catching people doing something right" into practice and instantly begin to obtain results. As they kept with it, recognition practices spread throughout their organization, becoming an integral part of the company's culture and a distinct competitive advantage for the organization.

As powerful as recognizing and rewarding desired performance is, through my work with hundreds of companies, I began to see that other workplace practices and activities that were not traditionally considered rewards could have an equally powerful impact on employee initiative, involvement, and commitment. I started collecting examples of practices that made people want to come to work, excited about doing their best, every single day.

I sought to discover organizations that *treated* people as though they were their most valuable asset—instead of just saying it was so. These organizations obtained impressive results and were more competitive precisely because of the way they treated their people. I found that such companies were special places where employees enjoyed coming to work, morale was strong and productivity was even stronger. In these companies, individuals brought their best thinking and ideas to the workplace on a daily basis, did what needed to be done without being told, and felt they had a significant impact in their jobs.

This book presents the results of my research. In the chapters that follow, you will find simple techniques and activities that can serve as extraordinary energizers. Whether you are looking for cost-saving ideas, improved decision making, enhanced employee initiative, or ways to retain your most valued employees, you'll find ideas that you can readily put into practice, which will make it easier to get the best from your employees each and every day.

Part I focuses on the individual, and gives energizing techniques that managers can use to enhance the one-on-one manager/employee relationship and the effectiveness of the individual employee.

Part II addresses team efforts and offers techniques that can be used to increase the effectiveness of any team, department, or group. More and more organizations today are turning to teams to get projects done; this section shows what leading companies are doing to achieve the best results from their teams.

Part III discusses the organization and shows techniques and systems for getting desirable results from employees throughout the entire organization.

In addition, throughout the book you will find highlights from recent research, quotes from business leaders, case studies of exceptional companies, and sample corporate vision statements that relate to the topic of energizing employees.

My hope is that as you read it, you will come to believe that what and how you communicate with your employees is as important as what you pay them, that involving employees in decisions that affect them will result in better decisions that are more readily implemented, and that the skills and training employees receive at work are as essential for their long-term relationship with the organization as the size of their last bonus. I know

that you will find examples and techniques throughout this book that can be readily implemented in your own workplace to make it—and everyone in it—a little more successful.

Bob Nelson
San Diego, California

PART I

ENERGIZING INDIVIDUALS

At the core of an energized workforce is the quality of the one-on-one relationships that individual workers have with their managers, and the trust, respect, and consideration that their managers show toward them on a daily basis. Getting the best out of workers is above all a product of the "softer" side of management—how individuals are treated, inspired, and challenged to do their best work—and the support, resources, and guidance that is provided by managers to help make exceptional employee performance a reality.

The work environment and the degree to which it serves to enable or inhibit individuals in getting work done is also important. Something as simple as sprucing up a drab workplace or holding an occasional morale-building celebration can make a difference. Providing schedule flexibility or the best equipment for getting the job done right may cost more, but can be money very well spent.

This section is about the kinds of things managers can do to energize employees. As you will see in the examples that follow, it doesn't necessarily take much to bring out the best in people: simply asking for their opinions, providing them with timely information that is important to them or involving them in decisions—especially when those decisions directly affect them or their jobs—can be very effective.

Building Morale

What can one person do to energize his or her employees, co-workers, or managers, and improve morale in the process? A lot! According to a recent survey by New York City-based consulting firm Towers Perrin, 75 percent of employees polled believe they can have a direct impact on their company's success and 72 percent derive a sense of accomplishment from their jobs.

Think about a particularly tough day you've had recently—maybe the copier jammed one time too many, or a customer decided to vent his or her anger at you. Just when it seemed that all was lost, your boss dropped by to thank you for doing a terrific job on an assignment that you are particularly proud of. Suddenly, your troubles with the copier and the angry customer were forgotten—replaced with the personal satisfaction of being recognized for a job well done.

During the busiest times of the year, executives at the Cigna Group, an insurance company headquartered in Hartford, Connecticut, personally push coffee carts around the office, serving drinks and refreshments to their frontline partners. As they serve, the executives coach and encourage their colleagues as well as hear about real consumer issues from those who know customer concerns the best.

> **"**People today are looking for much more than a paycheck. They want to be treated like human beings. That may sound obvious, but a lot of employers still don't get it.**"**
>
> MITCHELL THALL
> President, Epicure

Herb Kelleher, CEO and co-founder of Dallas-based Southwest Airlines, has discovered that by becoming personally involved in

The Importance of Connecting

How can managers tell when they are connecting with their employees? In his book *Getting Employees to Fall in Love With Your Company*, Jim Harris offers the following guidelines:

1. When you connect, employees feel free to speak up. They know their opinions matter.

2. Connected employees are confident that they will receive timely information concerning things in their particular area and the company at large.

3. Connection results in employee commitment. Employees who do not feel connected to their companies seldom offer the extra energy or ideas that are so essential to succeeding in today's marketplace.

4. You are connecting when you understand the needs of your employees. Mutual understanding between employees and management is the only way to attain the goals of high-quality, great service, and a fair profit.

the workplace and in the jobs that his employees do, he can unleash a tremendous amount of energy among his workers. For example, Kelleher often helps flight attendants serve beverages to customers when he flies on his airline.

President Tom McConnell of Boston's New England Securities Corporation urges his employees to try to solve problems themselves when they see them and to take pride in and "ownership" of the solution. To inject a dose of energy into his workforce, McConnell distributed customized T-shirts with the slogan "See it, Do it, Own it" to employees.

To ensure that employees know he has read their reports, Harry Seifert, CEO of New Oxford, Pennsylvania-based Winter Gardens Salad Company, stamps "Read by Harry" on reports and then routes them back to employees, often adding personal comments. According to Seifert, the quality of reports he receives has improved since he started using the rubber stamp.

Employees who have a sense of ownership of the products they produce are energized employees. Cooper Tires of Findlay, Ohio, has a long-standing tradition that is a great source of pride for its workers. In recognition of their contributions to the company, operators are allowed to stamp their names on the inside of the tires they produce.

———

The Dallas office of Ron McDougall, president of Brinker International, is filled with cow bric-a-brac, including cowbells and ceramic cow lamps. Why? It's his way of encouraging everyone in the southwestern-themed national restaurant chain to seek out and destroy any sacred cows that eat away at productivity and profit. McDougall calls this program "Cowabunga."

———

In many companies new-hires are shown to their desks, given a pile of reports to read, and expected to get right to work. At Hewitt Associates, a compensation-and-benefits firm headquartered in Lincolnshire, Illinois, new employees aren't taken for granted. "I joined the firm about six months ago as a writer/consultant in New Jersey," says new-hire Vernon Valentine. "I was surprised at the level of detail that had gone into the preparation for my arrival. The secretary had ordered all the supplies I would need—not just paper and pens, but schedule books and a wall calendar as well. One of the more experienced writers left a welcome note on my desk, along with a "survival kit" (including a candy bar and nerf ball) . . . and *everybody* came by my office to personally welcome me to the team. For the first two weeks or so, every day somebody

> **"**Give people a chance not just to do a job but to have some impact, and they'll really respond, get on their roller skates, and race around to make sure it happens.**"**
>
> ROBERT HAUPTFUHRER
> Chairman and CEO,
> Oryx Energy

"The highest achievable level of service comes from the heart, so the company that reaches its people's hearts will provide the very best service."

HAL ROSENBLUTH
CEO, Rosenbluth
International

made a point to stop by and ask me to lunch. Perhaps the most surprising, my name had been automatically added to the office softball roster—the folks who interviewed me had really listened."

To improve the morale of its drivers, Bar-Nunn Transportation of Granger, Iowa, provides them with two monthly publications— a newsletter and a four-hour cassette tape loaded with industry and company news, country music, information on company benefits, and personalized messages such as birthday announcements. Since creating these, the company has experienced a 35 percent reduction in its turnover rate.

When managers go out of their way to do something special for their employees, both managers *and* employees become energized. At Physio-Control, a producer of cardiac care equipment in Redmond, Washington, employees who attend fourth-quarter meetings are treated to a pancake breakfast served by senior managers. The employees are energized by being invited to attend the meeting and by the special effort made by managers to serve them.

Management at Advanced Micro Devices, a semiconductor producer located in Sunnyvale, California, keeps employee morale high by putting employees first. In the words of

CEO and founder Jerry Sanders, "If we take care of our people, products will be created, and profits will follow." This philosophy was put to the test when the company had to break its long-standing no-layoff policy. During a prolonged downturn in the computer chip market, Sanders and the rest of the company's management team did everything possible to cut costs and avert layoffs. The employees they did eventually have to lay off were offered very generous severance packages, a consideration which earned the respect of employees.

> **"If you show people you don't care, they'll return the favor. Show them you care about them, and they'll reciprocate."**
>
> LEE G. BOLMAN &
> TERRENCE E. DEAL
> *Leading with Soul: An Uncommon Journey of Spirit*

———

When Mike Warren became president of Alagasco of Birmingham, Alabama, the largest distributor of natural gas in the state, he had to overcome more than 130 years of tradition in order to break the "utility mind-set" and empower employees to make improvements in the way they did business. According to the Company's vice president of human relations, David Self, the mind-set was "If it worked last year or five or ten years ago, then don't fix it." As a way of sending a message to employees who held onto this mind-set Warren had a special rubber stamp made with the image of a dinosaur. Whenever he read any company document—a letter, memo, or proposal—that exhibited this mind-set, Warren stamped it with his dinosaur stamp, and returned it to the author.

———

All new employees want to feel they have an important role to play in an organization.

> **"Having a good time is the best motivator there is. When people feel good about a company, they produce more."**
>
> DAVE LONGABERGER
> CEO, The Longaberger
> Company

This is particularly true when one company buys another, and employees are uncertain of their roles in the new organization. Energizing companies meet this challenge by going out of their way to welcome the newcomers, and to quickly absorb them into the corporate culture. When AT&T acquired Kirkland, Washington-based McCaw Cellular Communications, all McCaw employees received packets that included coupons for AT&T discounts, a pamphlet of greetings from AT&T employees, the AT&T mission statement, a "welcome" video from AT&T executives, a poster and T-shirt emblazoned with the words "Who will lead the future of communications? We will," and a sheet of "We Will" stickers.

———

At Rosenbluth International, a Philadelphia-based corporate travel agency, employees can look forward to special company events such as Hawaiian Shirt Gonzo Friday, Hoagie Day, and the formal "Salmon-chanted Evening" during August's Associate Appreciation Month.

———

Energizing managers aren't afraid to tell their employees how much they appreciate them. When Ed Stewart, an employee of Dallas-based Southwest Airlines, turned down a better-paying job offer to stay with Southwest, CEO Herb Kelleher walked into his office and kissed him.

———

Doug Bergum, founder and CEO of Great Plains Software, an accounting software firm located in Fargo, North Dakota, walked onstage during one of the company's annual dealer conferences and discussed in great detail the mistakes he had made by prematurely bringing a software upgrade to market. He then proceeded to smash three fresh eggs on his forehead. This action energized his employees not only by injecting a note of humor in the proceedings but by bringing the CEO off a pedestal. By publicly admitting his mistakes, he showed that he's human too.

> **"**Disney knew you couldn't have a supervisor in the back room yelling at you and then walk through the front door and greet a guest with a big smile as if nothing were wrong.**"**
>
> SHARON HARWOOD
> Manager,
> Disney University

To show production workers that they are valued, Eriez Magnetics, a producer of magnetic laboratory equipment located in Erie, Pennsylvania, provides all their factory workers with engraved plates displaying their names and positions and posts them at employee workstations. According to CEO Chet Giermak, "People like to see their names up there. Everybody wants to feel needed and useful."

Celebrations play an important role in energizing employees and improving their morale. At the headquarters of Ben & Jerry's Homemade Ice Cream in Waterbury, Vermont, co-founder Jerry Greenfield coordinates such special events as "National Clash Dressing Day" and "Elvis Day," on which everyone is served greasy hamburgers.

> **❝Employees will be more receptive to formal, organization-wide programs if they believe that the company really cares about them on a personal, day-to-day basis.❞**
>
> ROSALIND JEFFERIES
> Rewards and
> Recognition Consultant

At the end of "Pump-It-Up Week"—a week dedicated to improving the morale of employees—workers at BookCrafters in Chelsea, Michigan, look forward to a Breakfast of Champions. Managers energize the company's employees by taking the time to personally serve them breakfast.

———

Whenever they achieve a major success, employees at Atlanta-based Corporate Resource Development, a sales and marketing services company, set off a siren to let all their coworkers know about it.

———

Employees at Apple Computers in Cupertino, California, often use kazoos instead of applause to show their approval (or disapproval) of speakers at company meetings.

———

Each employee at the Gap's Canadian Distribution Center in Brampton, Ontario, was asked to place a pushpin on the country of his or her birth on a world map permanently displayed in the lobby. The 64 employees placed pins in their 15 countries of origin, creating a visual display that energized by recognizing diversity through heritage.

———

The human resources department at Data General, a computer manufacturer in Apex,

North Carolina, has instituted a "fiscal New Year's celebration" that occurs in October of each year. The department energizes its employees by celebrating the prior year's accomplishments, making resolutions for the new year, and developing a list of the top ten things employees would like to see happen. According to human resources manager B.D. Sechler, "Everyone gets a good laugh out of it. It's a great way to set the tone for the coming year."

When employees at Douglas Aircraft Distribution and Services Company in Long Beach, California, generate $10,000, they are encouraged to ring a large brass bell.

Pioneer/Eclipse, a manufacturer of floor-cleaning equipment in Sparta, North Carolina, takes customers on tours of the company's plant. While there, they are introduced to the line workers who build the clients' products. Workers take pride in telling the customers about the part they play in creating the company's products.

Original Copy Centers in Cleveland, Ohio, welcomes all new employees to the team by giving them a set of personalized business cards. Says president Nancy Vetrone, "It's a very simple way to recognize each person as important. The company also prints an em-

The Vision Thing

Hartford, Connecticut-based diversified manufacturer, United Technologies Corporation offers these guidelines to help management and workers develop a shared vision:

- Communicate your views honestly and directly during discussions with employees about their performance.

- Make sure others have the information they need to do their jobs.

- Allow your employees to influence their own performance goals.

- Get out of your office: Be visible and accessible.

- Communicate a clear view of the long-range direction of the unit.

- Listen carefully and consider the opinions of others open-mindedly before evaluating them.

- Communicate high personal standards informally—in conversation, day-to-day contact, etc.

SUGGESTION BOX

☛ Set time at the end of a special day to celebrate the achievement of a department or company milestone. Ask individuals to share what their part of the project was, and to tell any humorous anecdotes. Serve ice cream, pizza, or doughnuts.

☛ Give out humorous certificates of recognition to acknowledge individual achievements.

☛ On a new employee's first day of work, make sure that his or her desk is ready and waiting—clean and stocked with office essentials such as paper, pens, stapler, and tape.

ployee yearbook that includes photos and personal information such as favorite music, best childhood memory, and 'My Role at Original.' Cost for the 110-person company? $1,600, with most of the production done in-house.

———

When cashiers told the store manager at a Wegmans supermarket in Rochester, New York, that they felt they deserved a special day in recognition of their hard work, the manager quickly agreed. Within a month, the store walls were covered with posters announcing "Cashier Appreciation Day." On that day each cashier received a flower and a free lunch.

———

After discovering that a lack of nighttime bus service was forcing some of his third-shift workers to spend up to 15 hours on site, Dwayne Greer, manager of an Essilor of America plant in Mexico, arranged for a local taxi company to pick them up and drop them off at their homes. Within one year, this inexpensive program transformed a tremendous turnover problem into the enviable challenge of having to manage a waiting list of employees and applicants eager to join the third shift at the optical lenses plant.

———

Domino's Pizza, which is headquartered in Ann Arbor, Michigan, conducts an annual Olympics that includes competition in the areas of veggie-slicing, driving, dough-making and catching, and, for administrative employees, telephone and interpersonal skills. The opportunity to show off their work skills energizes employees and improves morale.

———

Vice presidents at Nobel/Sysco, a food distribution company in Denver, conduct regular employee appreciation lunches where they cook and serve the food. As employees pass through the serving line, the vice presidents tell them how much they are appreciated.

———

Hewitt Associates, a benefits-and-compensation firm located in Lincolnshire, Illinois, puts its employees first. "Last fall my three-year-old son had open-heart surgery, my wife was confined to bed with a high-risk pregnancy, and our daughter was born prematurely," says employee Steve Peterson. "Even though I handled a heavy client load, Hewitt arranged for me to work part-time for three months, maintained my benefits, and installed a computer at home so I could be with my family as much as possible. At first, I was nervous about how this might affect my career. But the attitude here is that family comes first." When the company celebrated its 50th anniversary, the company hired two temporary employees to cover the reception area so that the regular receptionist could attend the party. Sue Kachnovitz, the receptionist, says, "It made me feel very good to know that even the little people are remembered."

———

> "It's no good saying you can't afford to look after your staff. You can't afford not to."
>
> JULIAN RICHER
> Founder, Richer Sounds

"The best way to inspire people to superior performance is to convince them by everything you do and by your everyday attitude that you are wholeheartedly supporting them."

HAROLD GENEEN
Former CEO, IT&T

Advertising agency Dahlin Smith White gives all its employees a small "art budget" to use in decorating their offices. The only rule is stated in this Salt Lake City company motto: "Do something wild!"

The Pinellas County, Florida, public school administrative offices have designated a small area where employees can drop off clothing for dry cleaning in the morning. A local dry cleaner picks it up and returns it by the end of the workday.

London-based graphic design agency, What If, has implemented the "James Brown Principle," a policy of doing things to make employees "feel good!" The James Brown Principle has brought What If employees many unusual benefits, including an open account at the local pub, fruit and vitamin deliveries to the office, and company-paid visits from a spiritual healer.

Charlotte, North Carolina, manufacturer Wilton Conner Packaging employs an experienced maintenance worker, who is available to help employees with household tasks—everything from painting houses to unclogging drains and even building on additions—all for the cost of supplies only. The company also provides a "Buck a Load" laundry service—for $1 a load, employees can drop off their laundry and have it washed, dried, and folded.

At Miami's Baptist Hospital, employees give themselves a break from the tension of the hospital environment by throwing a "Monotony Breaker Day" on minor "holidays," such as Oktoberfest or the birthday of a famous poet. Snacks, drinks, and room decorations all celebrate the day's theme, and employees are encouraged to drop by the party-room when it is convenient, to socialize or just relax and take a break.

———

Once a year, employees at meat-processing equipment manufacturer Townsend Engineering of Des Moines, Iowa, may send up to $50 worth of flowers to a friend or loved one at the company's expense.

———

At Sunnyvale, California's Advanced Micro Devices (AMD), management promotes teamwork and boosts morale by banning exclusive perks such as executive dining rooms and reserved parking spots.

———

Cincinnati, Ohio-based Roto-Rooter, a nationwide plumbing chain, holds an annual employee appreciation week. Each day of this special week is chock-full of activities, including an employee appreciation toast and reception, a catered hot breakfast buffet, employee-management dinners, and even ice cream delivered to employee desks by the company's president.

———

> 66Every single person you meet has a sign around his or her neck that says, 'Make me feel important.' If you can do that, you'll be a success not only in business but in life as well.99
>
> MARY KAY ASH
> Founder,
> Mary Kay Cosmetics

"The mistakes that people will make are of much less importance than the mistake that management makes if it tells them exactly what to do."

WILLIAM MCKNIGHT
Former CEO, 3M

Richard Anderson, CEO of Lands' End, a catalog retailer in Dodgeville, Wisconsin, believes that a company's fostering a good relationship with its employees is simply good business. "I think the first principle of the company, the foundation, is to treat all our people as we would like to be treated. This is not a company where people stand on titles or things like that. People talk to each other. People call me by my first name. The better they feel, the better their benefits, the better they're taken care of, the more we prosper. And we believe if our people feel good, their positive attitude comes out over the phone. It's kind of simple, but that's about the truth of it."

To recognize the difficulties presented to employees' families when workers are required to work long periods of overtime, Bur-Jon Steel Service Center of Springboro, Ohio, sends flowers and free dinner coupons directly to the workers' spouses or significant others along with a personal note of thanks.

When Hewlett-Packard in Palo Alto, California, closed its printed circuit board division, employees staged a New Orleans-style jazz-band funeral to help employees deal with the emotional loss. After a 30-minute eulogy recounting the history and achievements of the division, a symbolic coffin was buried, and the funeral became a celebration.

To demonstrate to all employees how important their jobs are, Anne Robinson, president and CEO of Windham Hill Records in Palo Alto, California, holds an hour-long meeting every Monday morning for all 30 employees at company headquarters. Everyone from the warehouse stocker to Robinson herself gives a two-minute summary of what he or she plans to accomplish in the upcoming week. According to Robinson, employees report more accurately than if a manager spoke for them, and they are instilled with a sense of pride in their work.

> **"**We can invest all the money on Wall Street in new technologies, but we can't realize the benefits of improved productivity until companies rediscover the value of human loyalty.**"**
>
> FREDERICK REICHHELD
> Director, Bain & Co.

———

When overnight shipper Federal Express of Memphis, Tennessee, took over Flying Tigers, an air freight company, the employees of Flying Tigers and their families were treated to a welcome that they will not soon forget. As they stepped off Boeing 747s chartered by FedEx for the event, the employees and their guests were greeted by cheering crowds of Federal Express employees as they walked a red carpet to the welcoming committee, which included the CEO of FedEx and the mayor of Memphis.

———

Empowerment, Independence, and Autonomy

Empowerment—giving employees the responsibility and the authority to get things done their way—can unleash tremendous amounts of worker energy. Employees want to feel that they are trusted and valued members of the organization. When they are granted independence and autonomy, not only can their supervisors concentrate on other issues, but the employees are able to make better decisions—and they're usually a lot happier on the job. When asked how his company was able to increase earnings by 246 percent—to $3.7 billion—Chrysler's chief executive officer, Robert Eaton, replied: "If I had to use one word, it's empowerment."

There's nothing that pumps up an employee's energy more quickly or more completely than when he or she is supported for showing personal initiative or for going out on a limb to provide better service or products to a customer. Smart businesspeople know that it makes sense to empower their workers—even if they make a mistake or two along the way. According to a Gallup survey of 1,200 U.S. workers, 66 percent of respondents say their managers have asked them to get involved in decision making, but only 14 percent feel they have been empowered to make those decisions. Don't just talk empowerment—give your employees real independence and autonomy!

What better way to energize an employee than to demonstrate, yourself, the power of individual initiative? One day, a new manager ran into the office of CEO Norm Brodsky of Perfect Courier in Brooklyn, New York, announced that the toilet was flooding, and asked what to do or who to call. Brodsky grabbed a mop and bucket from the closet and cleaned up the bathroom. To the surprised new manager Brodsky explained, "That's what we do here when the toilet floods. Next time, you'll know."

———

Management at Domino's Pizza, headquartered in Ann Arbor, Michigan, emphasizes its support of employees who act independently to further the goals of the company. It was therefore no surprise to them when a janitor who took an off-hours call at Domino's supply distribution center from a franchisee about to run out of pepperoni grabbed the keys to a truck, threw in a box of pepperoni, and drove several hundred miles to deliver the precious cargo and keep the store open.

———

At Chaparral Steel in Midlothian, Texas, workers are entrusted with extraordinary freedom to use company money and resources to improve work processes as they see fit. Two maintenance workers bought the parts necessary to invent and build a machine for strapping steel rods together at a cost of $60,000—almost $200,000 less than the cost of the old machines.

———

SUGGESTION BOX

☛ When an individual does a good job on an assignment, let him or her choose the next assignment.

☛ Whenever possible, allow flexibility in working hours. Focus on employee results, not presence.

☛ Allow high-performing employees to work at home and to set their own schedules.

> **The real impediment to productivity isn't the workers, union or non-union; it's management.**
>
> KEN IVERSON,
> Chairman, Nucor Corp.

To encourage employees to exercise initiative in their jobs and to take risks without fear of retribution, Richard Zimmerman, the chairman and CEO of Hershey Foods of Hershey, Pennsylvania, created a special award: the Exalted Order of the Extended Neck. According to Zimmerman, "I wanted to reward people who were willing to buck the system, practice a little entrepreneurship, who were willing to stand the heat for an idea they really believe in." The award has been given out on numerous occasions, including to a maintenance worker who devised a way to perform midweek cleaning on a piece of machinery without losing running time.

Two employees of Phelps County Bank in Rolla, Missouri, developed a proposal for creating a seniors banking program. The proposal—which included special checking and savings accounts, community "ambassadors," and more—was greeted with accolades by the company's management and was soon implemented.

Employees at Muni Financial Services in Temecula, California, can call a "Yes" meeting anytime by simply pushing the page button on their telephone. When such a meeting is called—to announce a new client, or to discuss strategy or financial results—*all* employees must attend. Tradition requires employees to share credit for successes and to end each meeting with a "one-two-three *yes!*" cheer.

Washington D.C.-based Telecommunications giant MCI encourages its employees to thrive on positive action rather than focus on mistakes. According to one executive, "At MCI we don't shoot people who make mistakes, we shoot people who don't take risks."

When the divisional general manager of Rockwell Semiconductor, in Newport Beach, California, raised the spending authority from $25 to $200, spending dropped by 60 percent. "Cutting costs wasn't the point," says the manager. "It was to quit treating them like kids. Now, with the $200 limit people say to themselves, 'Hey, that's a lot of money I'm responsible for.' They look at it as theirs."

All sales associates at Alcoa, Tennessee-based Parisian's department stores are encouraged to make independent decisions in solving customer complaints; the only person who can say no to a customer is the store manager. This policy energizes employees by empowering them to think for themselves, rather than deferring to management. Employees also learn to live by the company's first rule: Never let a customer leave unhappy.

When Lyondell Petrochemical CEO Bob Gower removed several layers of supervision, workers were given more authority and responsibility over their own jobs. Says employee Allen Reynolds, "Before, chain of

> **"**Ultimately, we're talking about redefining the relationship between boss and subordinate.**"**
>
> JACK WELCH
> Chairman, General Electric

66 The main thing that makes me happy about getting up in the morning and coming to work is the fact that I like what I do and I have freedom. I'm free to do my job, take complaints or recommendations to my supervisors, and I know they will listen. I can order my own parts, take care of everything, and carry it on through. It's a lot more pleasant to be in a job like that. 99

JERRY FORSYTHE
Senior Operator,
Chaparral Steel

command was the key phrase. You didn't do anything until you were told to do it. It was crazy because you already knew what you needed to do. Now we just react to what is going on, and do it." Lab technician Leticia Ligsay agrees that Houston-based Lyondell is a better place to work now that workers are empowered to make their own decisions. "We have the freedom to think. And it is fun."

Instead of subjecting customers to lengthy waits while performing price checks on unmarked items, cashiers at Dayton Hudson's Target retail chain in Minneapolis, Minnesota, are allowed to ask the customer if he or she knows what the price is and then, if the price seems reasonable, to enter it in the cash register without seeking approval from a supervisor.

Owner Katherine Barchetti assigns each of the salespeople at her clothing stores in Pittsburgh, Pennsylvania, responsibility for certain items of merchandise—a particular brand and style of belt, for example. Salespeople fully manage the product line they have been assigned, from buying and maintaining inventory to marketing and selling it.

Overnight shipper FedEx, headquartered in Memphis, Tennessee, has eliminated the practice of placing new-hires on probation. All employees are treated as fully participating partners from day one.

At aerospace parts manufacturer United Technologies Corporation, headquartered in Hartford, Connecticut, employees get involved in many ways. For example:

- Employees from all areas of the corporation team up and serve together on problem-solving productivity task forces.

- Production employees contact customers directly to identify and correct quality control problems.

- Production employees chair meetings to address issues of quality control, productivity, capital equipment plans, and customer relations.

- Customer letters and comments are shared with all employees immediately and regularly.

- Employees "stop production" when quality is not up to standard.

- Employees actively participate in plant tours and customer presentations.

- Employees visit vendors' facilities to learn more about their manufacturing processes, in order to improve incoming product quality.

At automobile maker Honda of America Manufacturing in Marysville, Ohio, workers are encouraged to become active participants in the decision-making process. According to

"Decisions must be made at the lowest possible level for management at the top to retain its effectiveness."

SAXON TATE
Managing Director, Canada
and Dominion Sugar

"Hire the best people and then delegate."

CAROL A. TABER
Publisher,
Working Woman

associate relations-manager Donnie McGhee, "It was mind-boggling for me to come here and see the amount of involvement of the general associate [employee] in problems and situations that I viewed as management-type issues. There is sharing of responsibility. The manager is there, but right alongside that manager you'll find a general associate. They're both out there, getting their hands dirty, problem-solving. Often it's difficult to make that separation between who is the manager and who is the general associate."

———

Nurses at San Diego's Mercy Hospital have been given the authority to perform numerous patient-related tasks, such as drawing blood and performing EKGs, formerly reserved for specialized technicians. This gain in autonomy has energized the nurses and improved patient care and has allowed management to cut six or seven layers of supervision down to three or four, and collapse thirty-five separate job descriptions down to only four.

———

Management at AT&T Universal Card Services in Jacksonville, Florida, allows employees to use their own judgment to waive late fees or raise customer credit limits on the spot. This has made the system more efficient and given employees a greater sense of control over their jobs.

———

Alex Dillard, executive vice president of Dillard Department Stores, headquartered in Little Rock, Arkansas, understands that a store manager knows his or her customers far better than anyone at corporate headquarters. So when he visits his 230 stores, he insists that the store managers locate merchandise where it will sell best and not just blindly follow corporate recommendations. By freeing its managers to do what they know is best, Dillard continues to be a profitable industry leader.

———

Employees at Microsoft headquarters in Redmond, Washington, are given tremendous latitude in deciding how to get their jobs done. Employees respond to this freedom by working with an intensity that is hard to find elsewhere. According to one employee, "You have everything you need to create just about anything, and the independence to decide exactly what to build."

———

The management team of Phelps County Bank in Rolla, Missouri, has long believed in giving its employees the authority to make decisions. They formed the Problem Busters committee—chartered to help untangle bottlenecks and deal with employee grievances—to encourage employees to solve their own problems.

———

Why Energize?

Here are six reasons to energize employees, adapted from the Web site of the Lone Star Chapter of the Employee Involvement Association:

1. Downsizing, rightsizing, and reengineering create environments in which employee trust must be rebuilt.

2. Employees today must be more self-directed and autonomous on the job.

3. Managers today must create supportive work environments to foster desired behaviors and outcomes.

4. The more "high-tech" our work environments become, the more "high-touch" managers must be with their employees.

5. A manager's limited time with his or her employees must be positive and meaningful.

6. All employees want to feel valued and appreciated for their work, their knowledge, and their skills.

> **❝I don't want people to sit there and passively accept leadership. I want them to become active in leadership, and that means giving them a constructive path to follow. I don't think managers should be glorified cheerleaders.❞**
>
> JACK STACK
> President and CEO,
> SRC Corporation

According to Ralph Stayer, CEO of Johnsonville Foods of Sheboygan Falls, Wisconsin, there are six truths about human behavior that must be grasped in order to empower employees to give their best performance. They are:

■ People want to be great. If they aren't, it's because management won't let them be.

■ The quality of performance begins with each individual's expectations. Influence people's expectations and you will influence how well they perform.

■ Expectations are driven partly by goals, vision, symbols, and semantics—and partly by the context in which people work, that is, by such things as compensation systems, production practices, and decision-making structures.

■ Managers' actions shape worker expectations.

■ Learning is a process, not a goal. Each new insight creates another new layer of potential insights.

■ The organization's results reflect me and my performance. If I want to change the results, I have to change myself first. This is particularly true for me, the owner and CEO, but it is also true for every employee.

———

CASE STUDY:
PROBLEM SOLVING AT GENERAL ELECTRIC

Chairman Jack Welch has led manufacturing giant General Electric to record sales and profits. With more than $60 billion in annual revenues, Fairfield, Connecticut-based GE is in the uppermost rank of industrial powers worldwide. From light bulbs priced at less than a dollar, to billion-dollar power plants, GE does it all.

Welch and his workers did not achieve this phenomenal success through the old-fashioned, "I'm the boss, you're the worker" style of management. Instead, Welch championed a whole new way of doing business—a way that is being copied in countless businesses around the world. Welch's system energizes GE employees by making them active, decision-making participants in the process. "We're going to win on our ideas, not by using whips and chains," Welch remarks.

His approach is, as he puts it, "to take out the boss element." By this he means that today's successful managers have to put aside the old roles of management—planning, organizing, implementing, and measuring—and adopt new roles such as counseling groups, facilitating the employee thought process, and winning resources for employees. Despite this shift from the old, clearly defined role of management to a new, "softer" approach, employee performance is still paramount. According to Welch, "The only ideas that count are the 'A' ideas. There is no second place. That means we have to get everybody in the organization involved. If you do that right, the best ideas will rise to the top."

A New Way of Managing

Welch's new management style consists of three key components: Work-Out, Best Practices, and Process Mapping.

Work-Out is a three-day session—conducted at a conference center or hotel—that brings together 40 to 100 employees picked by management from many different levels and parts of the organization. On the first day, a manager begins by roughing out an agenda, and then leaves. Next the group is broken into five or six teams guided by an outside facilitator. Each team chooses a

Continued on next page.

piece of the agenda to work on for the next day and a half. On the third day, the manager returns and each team makes its presentation. The manager has only three options: to agree on the spot, to disagree, or to ask for more information. Says GE manager Armand Lauzon, "I was wringing wet within half an hour. I was presented with 108 different proposals, and I only had about a minute to say yes or no to each one. . . ." However, Lauzon agreed to all but eight of his employees' proposals, which resulted in savings of more than $200,000 in a one-year period.

Work-Out proposals often save GE large amounts of time and money. As a result of one proposal, GE's hourly workers bid against another firm to build protective shields for grinding machines, and won. And at the GE-owned television network, NBC, another Work-Out proposal called for the discontinuation of a variety of useless forms, saving more than two million sheets of paper each year.

Best Practices involves studying other firms to find out the secrets of their successes. GE's initial study—involving eight firms that had achieved faster productivity growth than GE and were able to sustain the growth for ten years or longer—

included Ford, Hewlett-Packard, Xerox, Chaparral Steel, AMP, and three Japanese companies. In exchange for the opportunity for GE to learn these companies' management practices, GE agreed to share the results of the study with the participants and to let them ask questions.

Through the Best Practices study, GE learned that it was managing the wrong things and measuring the wrong results. According to business development manager George Zippel, "We should have focused more on *how* things got done than on *what* got done."

In **Process Mapping**, everyone who participates in a particular process gets together to define every single step, from beginning to end. The goal is to make sure that what management thinks should happen in a particular process really does. Process-mapping teams include not only GE managers and workers, but also customers and suppliers.

It took more than a month for the group that produces turbine shafts for jet engines to map out their process, and the map filled the walls of a conference room. However, by locating bottlenecks in the process, the team was able to cut production time in half and reduce its inventory by $4 million.

Crossing Boundaries

In addition to his three-part system of employee involvement, Welch is a big believer in encouraging employees to cross departmental and hierarchical boundaries to get their jobs done. "What we value most is 'boundarylessness,'" says Welch. "It's the ability to work up and down the hierarchy, across functions and geographies, and with suppliers and customers."

He adds, "When there are no limits to whom you'll see, where you'll go, what you'll touch, the results are remarkable. Everywhere we go, someone is doing something better. Finding that better idea is rewarded at GE."

> "Finding that better idea is rewarded at GE."
>
> JACK WELCH, Chairman

So how does GE train its quarter million or so employees in these new techniques of employee empowerment? The company's secret weapon is its Management Development Institute—also known as Crotonville because it's located in Crotonville, New York. At the "Harvard of Corporate America," each week 120 GE managers are offered classes that rival those offered by the nation's best graduate schools of business. Crotonville's course catalog—which is a hefty 160 pages long—offers a wide variety of classes in advanced management training, manufacturing, sales, and a basic economics course for engineers and English majors titled Eyawtkaf—Everything You Always Wanted to Know About Finance. (The tuition that GE charges its students' home departments also rivals the best and brightest MBA programs. It ranges from $800 for a half-week conference all new professional employees participate in to $14,000 for a four-week Executive Development Course.)

Not surprisingly, the star attraction at Crotonville is Welch, who drops in once a month to conduct question-and-answer sessions with GE managers. Because of the informal atmosphere, Welch has the chance to interact with employees from throughout the organization—many of whom he would normally never encounter during the course of business. According to Welch, these visits are "a great way to take the pulse of the organization." That he enjoys the sessions is readily apparent. Welch claims that he has rarely missed a month since becoming General Electric's chief executive officer.

66Nothing creates more self-respect among employees than being included in the process of making decisions.**99**

JUDITH M. BARDWICK
The Plateauing Trap

Any employee at the Ritz-Carlton Hotel Company, based in Atlanta, has the authority to do anything needed, and spend up to $2,000, to satisfactorily resolve a guest's complaint on the spot, no questions asked.

Reference International Software in San Francisco sets aside one day each week for its customer service representatives to work on projects of their own choosing. One employee programmed a demonstration disk; another started in-house software training classes. According to president Don Emery, the system "has benefited our company as much as it has our employees."

After completing customer service training, bus operators at San Diego Transit in San Diego, California, are given personalized business cards that can be given to customers to use as tickets for a free bus ride. Drivers can use their discretion to distribute the cards, resolving customer conflicts on the spot.

The manufacturing staff of the Longaberger Company, a producer of handcrafted items in Dresden, Ohio, elects its own floor supervisors. Employees also have the right to impeach the supervisors if things don't work out.

General Motors's successful Delco-Remy plant in Fitzgerald, Georgia, provides employees with autonomy in a wide variety of tasks and responsibilities. Workers at the plant typically:

- Are responsible for all safety and quality control issues.

- Do all the maintenance and minor repairs to their machines.

- Keep track of their own time.

- Handle all housekeeping duties.

- Participate in a pay-for-knowledge program.

- Participate in problem-solving teams.

- Have access to an unlocked tool room.

- Prepare and review their own budget.

- Determine staffing needs.

- Advise management on plant layout.

- Decide on new equipment purchases.

- Do all recruiting.

- Determine layoff patterns.

- Alternate as team leaders.

At Las Vegas's Mirage Treasure Island Hotels, management operates under a system of "planned insubordination." This means that all supervisors must explain to their employees not only what to do but *why* they should do it. If the

Common-Sense Principles

Here are the principles for empowering people from Diane Tracy's *10 Steps to Empowerment: A Common-Sense Guide to Managing People:*

1. Tell people what their responsibilities are.

2. Give them authority equal to their responsibilities.

3. Set standards of excellence.

4. Provide people with training that will enable them to meet these standards.

5. Give them knowledge and information.

6. Provide feedback on performance.

7. Recognize them for their achievements.

8. Trust them.

9. Give them permission to fail.

10. Treat them with dignity and respect.

> **"**Treat people as though they were what they ought to be and you help them become what they are capable of being.**"**
>
> GOETHE

explanation is not satisfactory, the employee can refuse to do the task. The hotels have a turnover rate that, at 12 percent, is less than half of the industry average.

———

At Johnsonville Foods in Sheboygan Falls, Wisconsin, employees who are promoted from merchandisers to salespeople hire their own replacements.

———

Management at steel processor Worthington Industries in Columbus, Ohio, has coffee and other refreshments always available to employees, who determine for themselves the best time to take their breaks.

———

At W.L. Gore & Associates, makers of Gore-Tex®, there are no titles or rules and there is no formal chain of command. While this is confusing for some employees, for many it is liberating. Says Tom Fairchild, an associate at the Newark, Delaware-based company, "Why go to someone with a title when you can go to someone with an answer?"

———

SRC Corporation, an engine rebuilder in Springfield, Missouri, assists employees in starting up and spinning off new businesses. In a recent year, the company funded five new companies created by company employees.

———

One-to-One Communication

Communication truly is the glue that holds an organization together. In high-performing organizations, employees on all levels are a vital link in the communication chain, and information is passed up and down the organization freely and quickly. Employees are entrusted with important financial information and they are included in the company's decision-making process. Well-informed employees are good and productive employees because they feel involved.

The positive effects of communicating vital company information to employees abound. For example, the manager of a Holiday Inn—one with an abysmal occupancy rate of 67 percent—decided to communicate the hotel's occupancy rate to all employees every day. Within 18 months, the rate had climbed to 85 percent, and employees were literally falling over themselves to greet customers, carry guests' bags, and generally be helpful and friendly. Without a doubt, employees who are "in the loop" are employees who are an energized and vital part of the organization.

To open channels of communication between workers and upper management, each of the ten officers and seven directors of Viking Freight System in San Jose, California, spend 25 percent of each year visiting all 4,000 of their employees, scattered throughout eight different states.

> **The most motivating thing one person can do for another is to listen.**
>
> Roy Moody, President, Roy Moody & Associates

> **❝**Ask people what they want to do. The workplace offers so many opportunities, and when we pair them with the right people, the results are amazing.**❞**
>
> CHERYL HIGHWARDEN,
> Consultant, ODT Inc.

Once a month, a manager at the Mirage Hotel in Las Vegas asks her staff, "What one thing can I do better for you?" After listening to and acknowledging the employees' ideas, she tells them one thing they can do better for her that month. This technique builds communication between all employees while focusing on continuous improvement.

———

Employees at California State University, Bakersfield, use their computer e-mail system to "tattle" on co-workers caught doing a good deed. When someone goes out of their way to help students, instructors, or staff, an employee sends out an "I caught so-and-so" message to all workers. Not only is word of the good deed communicated to all employees, but the employees who are reported on are energized by the positive attention from their co-workers.

———

Corporate executives at Wal-Mart, headquartered in Bentonville, Arkansas, spend the majority of each week flying from store to store to report on overall business, meet with groups of associates, solicit their ideas, and generally lead everyone in "the Wal-Mart cheer." The main reason for these trips is so that executives can gather worker ideas and maintain open communication throughout the organization.

———

To quickly bring new employees into the company's culture and to ensure that they don't get lost, Infinicom, an office-equipment distributor in Phoenix, Arizona, requires every new employee to seek out and hold a one-to-one discussion with each of the company's top managers. Not only do the new recruits quickly learn what is expected of them, but they also get to make a personal connection with the company's management team.

When chairman Rafael Rubio drops in on workers at the various locations of his San Diego-based Rubio's Home of the Fish Taco fast-food chain, he pumps them for ideas on how to improve the business. "You can have the best product in the world," says Rubio, "but you have nothing if you don't have the right people."

To let employees know how the company is doing, Jay Johnson of Crest Microfilm in Cedar Rapids, Iowa, holds a monthly employee communication session. The sessions are catered and Johnson varies the menu according to what he has to report. Employees know if it's pizza, the news could be better. If it's prime rib, company profits are really something to talk about.

To break down communication barriers between managers and workers, a large Canadian forest products company instituted a series of 30 dinners over the course of a year. At

Mutual Understanding

Employees appreciate supervisors who understand their needs. Here are five tips for establishing empathy with employees, as stated in *Entrepreneur* magazine:

■ Use body language to show that you are listening.

■ Show interest with your facial expressions.

■ Affirm your understanding verbally.

■ Ask for clarification.

■ Use "we" and "us" rather than "I" and "you" whenever possible.

> 66The exact words that you use are far less important than the energy, intensity and conviction with which you use them.99
>
> JULES ROSE
> Vice President,
> Sloan's Supermarkets

each dinner, ten employees and their spouses spend time socializing with their bosses. After the meal, there is a long and intense question-and-answer session about all aspects of the business. According to the president, "By the end of the evening I often see a remarkable change in attitude on the part of even the crustiest of the union guys."

To prevent miscommunication between management and employees, Palmer Reynolds, CEO of Phoenix Textile Corporation, an institutional linens distributor located in St. Louis, started hosting monthly breakfasts. Every month, Reynolds invites one employee from each of the company's five departments to join her for breakfast at a local restaurant. Because employees get to know her, and each other, they are often better able to work out problems. For example, at one such breakfast, the sales department learned about production department quotas, helping end a long-standing tug-of-war between the two groups. Due in part to improved communication and coordination, the company grew from $1.4 million in annual revenues to $24 million in only six years.

Vickers, a manufacturer of hydraulic pumps and motors in Jackson, Mississippi, conducts regular "roundtable" discussions with representatives from top management and various employees to discuss current problems, continuous improvement, and creative ideas.

This does more than demonstrate to employees that management cares about them: The company collects a lot of good ideas that can be readily implemented.

———

When Ed Carter became president of the Chicago office of Harza Engineering, he asked 30 top employees to complete a detailed survey that became the basis for a follow-up in-depth, 90-minute one-on-one discussion. He also scheduled weekly lunches, 10 employees at a time, with the other 140 staff members, effectively building connections with every employee in less than 12 weeks.

———

There are many ways for an organization's leader to communicate his or her beliefs to a team of employees. When Ron Peterson called his first employee meeting as the new CEO of Florida Forest Products, a building and specialty lumber company in Largo, Florida, he opened the meeting by discussing "Twelve Things I Believe In." Peterson's list included fairness, integrity, caring, sharing, and earning an honest profit.

———

Managers at Blanchard Training and Development in Escondido, California, conduct regular "one-on-one" meetings with their employees—a 15- to 30-minute meeting at least once every two weeks. The meetings set a minimum acceptable standard for "face" time with

> **"Employees deserve to know what's up and will handle the responsibility better than you imagine."**
>
> NANCY K. AUSTIN
> Management Consultant

SUGGESTION BOX

☛ *Make a point of getting together with the employees you interact with the least.*

☛ *When you assign a new project to an individual, schedule a specific time to review his or her progress.*

☛ *Enter and leave your facility through a variety of entrances and exits so that you interact with people you wouldn't otherwise see.*

☛ *Spend more time with employees during stressful times such as layoffs, major projects, or cost reductions. Energize them with pep talks or upbeat memos.*

☛ *Drop in on your employees from time to time.*

each employee and are a terrific way to make sure employees are getting the information they need and want, because the *employee* sets the agenda for each meeting. The company makes One-on-One forms available to all employees to help them prepare for these meetings. The agenda can range from questions about job assignments to discussions of strategic direction, resources and planned initiatives, to career and skill development.

———

Whenever Todd Arwood, senior manager of training and development for Rally's Hamburgers, based in Louisville, Kentucky, drops in at one of the chain's many fast-food restaurants, he makes a point of introducing himself to each and every employee. His caring enough about them to take the time to introduce himself and learn their names really energizes employees.

———

President Scott Mitchell of Mackay Envelope in Minneapolis, Minnesota, holds a one-on-one, 20-minute discussion with every employee every year to discuss ideas, improvements, or whatever is on the employee's mind. Mitchell devotes more than 170 hours to this task every year, an investment that he sees as time well spent.

———

At Armstrong Machine Works, located in Three Rivers, Michigan, either the plant's general manager or the controller personally delivers paychecks to some 300 workers each week. Why? According to company CEO David Armstrong, "We want everybody to have a chance to be heard. While we have an open-door policy, not everybody feels comfortable walking into the corner office. By having an officer of the company hand out paychecks, everyone is assured that at least once a week, he'll have a chance to ask a question, voice a concern, or suggest an idea to one of the people in charge."

Workers and management at Acipco (American Cast Iron Pipe Company) of Birmingham, Alabama, have an extraordinarily open relationship, and management works hard to keep the lines of communication open. This openness has led many employees to refer to their co-workers—from the top of the organizational chart to the bottom—as "family." Foreman Ray Clayton, a 35-year employee, says, "I really like the word 'family' because I feel that way. I have always felt that the people in high places here communicate with the people out in the shop, and I still believe they care for me. I know that I can go to talk to any of them, whether it's the head of the company, the head of the medical department, or whoever, and there's always a person there who's going to listen to your problems and do something about them. They're part of the Acipco family—and not someone to run and hide from."

> **"Handle every single transaction with each and every person, no matter who that person is, as if you will have to live with that person in a very small room for the rest of your life."**
>
> MICHAEL MESCON
> Founder and Chairman,
> The Mescon Company

CASE STUDY:
INTEL TELLS ALL

Along with IBM, Microsoft, and Apple, Intel Corporation is one of the major players in today's personal computer market. Intel invented the brain of the personal computer—the microprocessor—and currently owns 75 percent of the microprocessor market worldwide. This invention and its refinements have made Intel one of the most successful companies in the world, with $5.2 billion of operating income on $20.8 billion in sales in 1996.

Organized Common Sense

Intel wouldn't be where it is today, however, without an energized and involved workforce. Critical to Intel's success is the vision of the company's president, Andy Grove. And critical to Grove's vision is a policy of communicating as much information to as many employees as possible. "Management is about organized common sense," he says. "We communicate and communicate and communicate, at every level, in every form. Anyone can ask anybody any question. We have probably shaken loose a lot of bad ideas that way." Grove calls this policy "intellectual honesty"—workers telling each other and their bosses what they really think, regardless of the consequences.

While this approach may at times become confrontational, the advantage is that workers and managers alike are encouraged to drop the barriers to communication that often get in the way of good ideas.

Grove conducts a half-dozen or so open forums every year at different Intel locations. "I go somewhere and people fill a cafeteria. I start by showing a few slides and then hands go up and there are questions. I find these open forums with employees far more stimulating, in terms of the variety and incisiveness of the questions, than meetings with security analysts," he reports.

Another, more novel approach for communicating involved inserting slips of paper stating the company's goals inside fortune cookies. The cookies were passed out to employees at Intel's Sunnyvale, California, headquarters, and contained these two messages:

1. **Job 1.**
2. **Make the PC "it."**

The first message refers to Intel's goal of maintaining and strengthening its position as the world's number-one manufacturer of microprocessors. The second represents its goal of making the personal computer *the* key tool of the Information Age.

Another way that Intel has supported intellectual honesty, improved employee communication, and encouraged ongoing employee involvement is by abolishing the traditional closed-door office. At Intel, all employees—from chairman Gordon Moore on down—work in open cubicles. Whenever Grove is in his cubicle, *any* employee is welcome to drop in and speak with him. Intel has found that using cubicles for everyone breaks down barriers between managers and workers, as well as between different departments and work units.

Involvement and Initiative

Grove has nine management tips that demonstrate his commitment to employee involvement.

■ Motivation comes from within. The most a manager can do is create an environment in which motivated people can flourish.

■ A good coach takes no personal credit for the success of the team. He or she has played the game and understands it completely and is tough enough to get the very best performance the team can give.

■ Think about what you have to do today to solve—and avoid—tomorrow's problems.

■ Do everything within your power to provide co-workers with the best possible service.

■ Time is your one finite resource; remember that when you say yes to one thing you will have to say no to something else.

■ Schedule one hour every day to deal with the inevitable interruptions in a planned, organized manner.

■ Performance reviews are absolutely necessary.

■ To gather information about a corporate division or department, go on an unannounced visit and observe what's going on.

■ If an employee is not doing his job, there are only two possible explanations. Either he can't do it or he won't. To determine which, apply the following test: If the person's life depended on doing the work, could he do it? If the answer is yes, the problem is motivational. If the answer is no, the problem is lack of ability.

> 66When I first joined corporate America, the person in the corner office was a hallowed big guy with a loud bark and a very nasty bite. Now everything has changed. You have to be more like NBA coach Pat Riley, warm and motivating.99
>
> BRIAN RUDER
> President, Heinz U.S.A.
> Retail Products

To get to know her staff better and to exchange ideas, each week Connie Thede, manager of purchasing and stores for Muscatine Power & Water in Muscatine, Iowa, takes a different member of her staff out to lunch. According to Thede, "It has given me a tremendous opportunity to get to know them on a personal level outside the workplace, and it appears to be a real morale booster."

To keep in touch with both frontline employees and customers, the executive staff of Home Shopping Network, headquartered in St. Petersburg, Florida, can be found answering incoming customer calls. By helping out in this way they experience firsthand the role of frontline employees and better understand their needs.

The idea of open communication with employees was so important to Jerre Stead when he was appointed president of AT&T's Global Business Communications Systems unit a few years ago, that he had the lock removed from the door to his office, and has made it known that he is available to anyone who wants his "ear."

Fargo Electronics, based in Eden Prairie, Minnesota, established an electronic newsletter updated daily to share sales and production figures, customer feedback, and profit-sharing updates with employees. At the end of each workday, department heads send information into the company's e-mail system. The messages are collected in a file that is printed out and posted in the break room.

———

Hatim Tyabji, president and CEO of Veri-Fone, a manufacturer of financial transaction automation products based in Redwood City, California, prescribes the following five axioms for effective management:

■ Don't expect effective on-line communication without extensive face-to-face communication.

■ There's no such thing as giving people "too much" information.

■ Business is personal—people commit themselves to other people, not to organizations.

■ Small gestures send big signals—especially when they relate to core principles.

■ The essence of leadership is authenticity.

———

The Michigan Retailers' Association in Lansing threw a series of catered staff breakfasts on the Friday morning following each of five board of directors meetings. The breakfasts were used to share information and update staff on major policy actions and organizational developments.

———

Once a year, employees at XA Systems, a software developer in Los Gatos, California, have a one-on-one conversation with their

> ❝Whenever new technology is introduced…there must be a counter-balancing human response—that is, high touch—or the technology is rejected. The more high tech, the more high touch.❞
>
> JOHN NAISBITT
> *Megatrends: Ten Directions Transforming Our Lives*

> **66** An individual without information cannot take responsibility; an individual who is given information cannot help but take responsibility. **99**
>
> JAN CARLZON
> Former President and CEO,
> Scandinavian Airlines
> System

boss's boss. Employees are asked how things are going and if there is anything they need to do a better job. According to president Lacy Edwards, "It gives staff a legitimate opportunity to discuss problems and explore other in-company job possibilities without going around somebody."

To facilitate communication with employees in its many branches nationwide, executives at Staples, an office supply company headquartered in Framingham, Massachusetts, meet quarterly with employees at each of the chain's stores to discuss company performance and priorities. Employees are encouraged to ask questions and make suggestions, the results of which are published a month later in a booklet distributed to all employees.

Mike Allred, CEO and president of Visual Information Technologies, a graphics imaging company in Dallas, holds dry runs of presentations to his board of directors with his staff of 90 employees. This helps employees stay in touch with key organizational issues and proposals. They also ask tough questions that better prepare Allred for the real thing.

Todd Arwood, senior manager of training and development for Rally's Hamburgers, a fast-food chain headquartered in Louisville, Kentucky, builds energy, initiative, and involvement in the corporation by soliciting ideas for whatever project he is working on. Instead of relying on himself alone, Arwood creates a quick questionnaire and then phones employees at various levels around the country to get their insights and perspectives. Not only do the employees that Arwood surveys feel like they are an integral part of the team, but the practice also allows Arwood to make the smartest and most realistic decision possible.

———

CEO Hal Rosenbluth of Rosenbluth International, a chain of travel agencies headquartered in Philadelphia, is accessible to all his employees through an 800-number "voice-mail box." Employees are encouraged to call in with suggestions, problems, or praise, and about seven employees do so every day.

———

At the Walt Disney World Dolphin Hotel in Orlando, Florida, each manager hosts "5-minute chats" with 10 employees they don't directly manage every month as a way to be in better touch with staffers. Managers ask employees how their jobs are going and if there is anything they can do to help them.

———

Soliciting Suggestions

One of the best ways to involve employees in an organization, and to energize them in the process, is through the collection of employee suggestions. Various systems and programs—known by a wide variety of names, including total quality management, continuous improvement, or simply the good old suggestion box—encourage workers to make suggestions that will improve a company's products and services while reducing costs.

But employee suggestions don't just help the company: They also help the employees who make the suggestions by improving working conditions, removing the organizational hurdles that get in the way of workers' doing excellent work, and giving employees a measure of control over their jobs.

It's important for employees to know that their suggestions are taken seriously and that they can make a big difference. By carefully reviewing employee suggestions, and quickly implementing those that have merit, management sends a message to employees that they are valued.

> **"One percent improvement in 1000 things, rather than 1000 percent improvement in one thing."**
>
> TOM PETERS
> Management Guru

At Lincoln Electric, a manufacturer of arc-welding equipment located in Cleveland, Ohio, employees are *very* motivated to make cost-saving suggestions to management—and management is *very* motivated to energize its workforce by adopting those suggestions. Lincoln workers submit 200 to 300 suggestions every month. "We probably have more innovative ideas coming from our people than any other company I know of," says former CEO George Willis. "I think it's because we reward people for their contributions. . . . Over the years people have built up a basic trust that management is going to be fair in dividing the profit of the company among those who have produced it."

———

Organizations energize their employees when they quickly implement suggestions—it shows they value the input. It doesn't hurt that the suggestions often make employees more efficient and effective. At American Strap in Diamond City, Arkansas, an employee suggested a new way to stitch a piece of leather. The new method, which saved 15 seconds per piece, added up to a staggering 833 hours of annual savings when multiplied by the 200,000 pieces produced each year.

———

An employee suggestion program at Preston Trucking in Preston, Maryland, brought in almost 8,000 suggestions in a recent year, and the vast majority of them were implemented. All employee suggestions—including ideas that ranged from repainting the lines in the parking lots, to placing a rubber mat in front of the ice machine to prevent employee slips and falls, to purchasing rechargeable batteries for pagers— are printed in the company newsletter. Preston's management responds to and appreciates its employees' suggestions, and employees are energized because they know that their ideas are heard and valued.

———

SUGGESTION BOX

☞ Encourage employees to make suggestions that improve either the workplace or service to your customers.

☞ When employees make suggestions, ensure that they are responded to and acted upon quickly.

☞ Encourage any idea, no matter how small. Sometimes you have to get through simple suggestions before employees begin offering more significant ones.

☞ Publicly acknowledge the individuals who make suggestions and the improvements that result.

Getting Employees Involved

Management consultant Bernie Sander has developed the following list of ways to involve employees and to elicit their ideas for improvements:

■ Challenge employees to seek out empowering role models in the workplace.

■ Inspire supervisors to embrace new ideas.

■ Encourage breakthrough thinking.

■ Promote creativity as a learnable skill.

■ Advocate continuous improvement.

■ Foster the effective management of ideas.

■ Strive to make the interactions between employees and customers as positive as possible.

■ Adopt what is new.

■ Train, train, train.

The elimination of fear within an organization can go a long way toward energizing employees. Breakfast meetings called to solicit employee suggestions at Rockwell's Semiconductor Division in Newport Beach, California, were stilted until employees realized they weren't going to get into trouble with their bosses for discussing areas that needed improvement and that the president of the company was acting on their suggestions. The result was an outpouring of new ideas—not only at the breakfasts, but throughout the organization.

Obtaining the ideas of company outsiders can be an important ingredient in generating new employee suggestions. At Beckman Instruments, a maker of scientific lab instruments in Fullerton, California, employees on the manufacturing floor are encouraged to speak with visitors to the plant about the continuous process improvements they make on the job. These discussions often lead to valuable new suggestions.

When employees understand the workings of the entire organization—not just the small part they work for—they are able to generate suggestions that cross departmental lines and have a greater impact. Ford Motor Company, headquartered in Dearborn, Michigan, takes its workers on their tourist plant tour to help them see how their specific jobs fit into the organization's big picture, and to generate more and better suggestions for improvement.

The president of Pizza Hut, a fast-food chain headquartered in Dallas, asked employees how to eliminate needless paperwork and other routine tasks, and how to improve their working conditions. The response to the suggestions that came in resulted in a company with fewer layers of management and less corporate paperwork—an energizing outcome for the employees, who now had less bureaucracy to get in the way of their doing their jobs.

> **❝The only ideas that count are the A ideas. There is no second place. That means we have to get everybody in the organization involved. If you do that right, the best ideas will rise to the top.❞**
>
> JACK WELCH
> Chairman, General Electric

Acknowledging the importance of employee suggestions, management at Clinch River Corporation's Harriman, Tennessee, paperboard plant, gives each employee a special pocket notebook in which to record suggestions.

In one year, employees at Hughes Aircraft in Los Angeles generated more than 23,000 ideas. The company's management demonstrated its respect for its employees by adopting most of them—resulting in savings of $477 million.

In some organizations, employees are reluctant to submit suggestions because they are afraid that they may be punished for doing so. To counter this reluctance, Xerox Corporation in Stamford, Connecticut, encourages its employees to submit their comments anonymously through its "Comment" card system. Responses to Comment cards are printed in one of the company's many publications, showing employees

Before Their Time

In their classic 1964 *Harvard Business Review* article "Democracy Is Inevitable," Philip Slater and Warren G. Bennis found that a *system of values* is critical to organizational effectiveness. Slater and Bennis forecast the enlightened, participative organization of today. This organization has the following characteristics:

1. Full and free communication regardless of rank or power.

2. A reliance on consensus rather than coercion or compromise.

3. Influence based on technical competence and knowledge rather than on the vagaries of personal whims or prerogatives of power.

4. An atmosphere that permits and even encourages *expression* of emotions as well as task-oriented behavior.

5. A bias that accepts the inevitability of conflict between the organization and the individual but is willing to cope with and mediate it on rational grounds.

that management takes their suggestions seriously, and doesn't "blame the messenger."

At Penton Publishing in Cleveland, Ohio, one employee suggested a casual dress day on Fridays. After a vote by all employees, Penton decided to define "casual day" as any day in which an employee wasn't going to meet with customers. Not only was one employee listened to, but the entire company benefited from the suggestion.

At McCormick and Company, a spice purveyor located in Hunt Valley, Maryland, one employee was energized when the company adopted his suggestion to purchase a key ingredient in bulk instead of by the bag, saving the company $30,000 in purchasing costs.

At AT&T Universal Card Services, the nation's second-largest issuer of credit cards, based in Jacksonville, Florida, the company's employee suggestion system yields 1,200 ideas a month and has saved the company millions of dollars. An employee suggestion to move 2,500 boxes of credit data entry records from an independent vendor to the company's record retention center resulted in savings of more than $25,000 in the first year. By implementing another employee suggestion, to convert all training documents from a paper-based to an electronic format, the company promoted its goal of a paperless work environment and saved almost $20,000 in the process. When another employee suggested cutting delivery of business forms back from four to three a day, the company saved $8,500 in the first year. Not only do suggestions such as these help the company's bottom line, they make employees more effective and more involved in the workplace.

Mike Warren, president of Alagasco, a gas company in Birmingham, Alabama, started an employee suggestion program called "Hey, Mike!" to get workers involved in expressing their ideas for improving the company. Warren distributed "Hey, Mike!" cards, attached to posters, throughout the organization. In the first month of the program, he received 100 cards back with employee suggestions. Following through on his commitment to the employees, Warren answered every one of them, implementing many employee-suggested improvements along the way.

At the world's largest manufacturer of farm machinery, John Deere of Moline, Illinois, employees make suggestions that will improve efficiency and reduce costs, because they know their ideas will be considered. After noticing how much time he wasted walking from one part of the plant to another to obtain replacement parts or to check the status of certain items, welder Gary Versluis requested and received a cellular phone to use at his workstation

SUGGESTION BOX

☞ Set up a prominent and easily accessible location where employees can post problems and others can post their proposed solutions.

☞ Use the Delphi method of problem solving, in which individuals respond to problems through anonymous, written responses to questionnaires prepared and circulated by administrative staff.

☞ Publicly recognize the positive impact on operations of the solutions employees devise for problems.

> **"**Unless we can involve our people in running our company, we're not going to be successful.**"**
>
> ROBERT HAAS,
> CEO, Levi Strauss & Co.

on the assembly line. In so doing, Deere's management gave Versluis the ability to become more efficient and more effective, while tapping his creativity and reinforcing his commitment to the organization.

———

Ed Woolard, former chairman of DuPont, which is headquartered in Wilmington, Delaware, was known for frequently asking employees questions such as "What would you do if you were in my job?" The result was many fresh, innovative ideas, unencumbered by the traditional restraints imposed on employees by the company's hierarchy, and higher morale in the ranks.

———

Encouraging Creativity

Energized employees are creative employees. When they are engaged in the operations of an organization, employees will voluntarily seek out new ways to address and solve problems. The best organizations find ways to give their employees the time, support, and tools they need to stimulate creative thinking. Unfortunately, the hurried pace at many organizations leaves precious little time for employees to just think and create. In fact, it's not unusual for employees to skip their lunch breaks or to stay well into the evening just to keep up. In such workplaces, it's especially important for employees to be given opportunities to relax—to share a laugh with their co-workers or just get away from the office for a bit.

At 3M (Minnesota Mining & Manufacturing) in St. Paul, employees are encouraged to develop and implement new products. Professional staff members whose ideas are given the nod by management build their own businesses within the company. Those who are successful in their efforts are given promotions and pay raises. There is no penalty for those who are not successful. Employees are energized by the opportunity to see their ideas come to fruition, and a large portion of the company's sales now come from products introduced through this program.

> **❝One of the stepping stones to a world-class operation is to tap into the creative and intellectual power of each and every employee.❞**
>
> HAROLD A. POLING
> Former Chairman and CEO,
> Ford Motor Company

SUGGESTION BOX

☞ Brainstorm with your employees. Follow these four rules:

☞ Encourage all ideas and refrain from evaluating or criticizing them.

☞ To get to the best solution, the wilder and crazier the ideas the better.

☞ Quantity, not quality, of ideas is most important.

☞ Encourage new combinations and improvements of old ideas.

☞ Allow employees to pursue their ideas.

Accounting-software developer SBT Corporation in Sausalito, California, gives its receptionists petty cash to use for stocking the front desk with yo-yos, candy, and toys. The receptionists are relaxed and happy—a feeling that rubs off on visitors and clients.

———

According to *Industry Week* magazine, Odetics, the robot maker based in Anaheim, California, is "the wackiest place to work in the United States." It is not uncommon for the company's employees to take part in all kinds of nutty, routine-breaking activities, including telephone-booth stuffing contests, bubble-gum blowing, and a '50s day, featuring a sock hop that starts at 6:00 a.m. The company also sponsors programs in stress management, acupressure, and yoga, which help employees to relax while unleashing their creativity.

———

One day, to make a break from the usual office routine, Jim Carpenter, owner and CEO of Wild Birds Unlimited, a wild-bird supplies company in Carmel, Indiana, stopped work and took the entire staff out for ice cream cones and a birdwatching nature walk in a local park.

———

Many companies find it useful to attempt to gauge the creativity of employees *before* they are hired. Before they may be considered for hire, applicants to Southwest Airlines in Dallas must provide a satisfactory answer to the question, "Tell me how you recently used your sense of humor in a work environment."

When William T. Quinn, Jr. of W.T. Quinn, a publishing company in Somerset, New Jersey, hands out bonuses to his employees, he urges them to be creative and spend the money on something fun. Why? According to Quinn, "It helps relieve job stress—saving up bonuses for a television set wouldn't do that."

Workweeks at the Longaberger Company, a maker of handcrafted items in Dresden, Ohio, are typically 35 hours long, and there is an unwritten rule that, if possible, up to a quarter of each workday should be dedicated to having fun. Employees are energized by the fact that management trusts them to get their work done and by the opportunity to have fun at work.

To spur their creativity, researchers at electronics manufacturer Hewlett-Packard, headquartered in Palo Alto, California, are given access to 24-hour laboratories and are urged to devote 10 percent of their time to personal pet projects.

At Rosenbluth International in Philadelphia, employees occasionally receive a packet containing construction paper and a box of crayons and are asked to draw a picture of what the com-

Keep It Fresh

Innovation is the life-blood of a successful, growing organization. Here are some simple tips for maintaining a fresh perspective with your employees or co-workers:

1. Encourage employees to work outside of the rigid constraints of the organization.

2. Cultivate creativity.

3. Encourage initiative.

4. Allow employees to set aside time to think and plan.

5. Reward risk taking.

6. Encourage employees to learn a variety of skills.

7. Encourage them to ask questions.

8. Be accessible.

9. Hire smart people.

10. Hire a diverse group of individuals.

> 66You can dream, create, design, and build the most wonderful place in the world . . . but it requires people to make the dream a reality.99
>
> WALT DISNEY

pany means to them. This simple exercise unleashes creativity and energy by allowing employees to express themselves in new ways. The technique has proven so effective that Rosenbluth now sends paper and crayons to its clients, too.

———

Hallmark Greeting Cards in Kansas City, Missouri, bankrolls a creativity center stocked with clay, paint, and other art materials to help the company's creative staff think up ideas for the 21,000 different greeting card designs it publishes each year. Hallmark's staff is energized by the freedom to create, and the company reaps the benefit in exciting new ideas.

———

In an effort to recharge the staff's "batteries" and to boost their creativity, management at Eclipse, a manufacturer of products and systems for energy, fluid flow, and environmental markets located in Rockford, Illinois, takes employees out of their "comfort zones" and places them in new, creative situations. Says vice president of human resources, John Myers, "We've had welders and design engineers taking art classes, and painting pictures to put on their refrigerators at home."

———

Although OurTown Television Productions of Saratoga Springs, New York, isn't able to offer its employees the same high salaries as its competition, it *does* offer them jobs custom-tailored to the individual interests of each worker. For example, the company's story coordinator is also the staff welder because he told one of OurTown's founders that he loved welding. Most OurTown employees make less money than their counterparts in the industry, but they love their jobs more.

———

To reduce stress among employees, the Los Angeles office of the Chiat Day advertising agency hangs punching bags with pictures of executives painted on them in the break room.

———

> 66A strong record on employee relations is generally an indication of forward-thinking executives thinking creatively about running a business.99
>
> STEVEN LYDENBERG
> Research Director,
> Kinder, Lydenberg,
> Domini & Co.

Training and Development

The best organizations recognize that providing employees with opportunities to learn pays dividends for both the organization and the employees. The organization gets better-skilled workers who are more versatile and flexible in their assignments, and employees get the opportunity to learn new skills, gain new ways of viewing the world, and meet and network with co-workers. The ability of employees to break out of their day-to-day routines is very energizing in itself. And when employees are given opportunities to learn and better themselves within the organization, it can electrify an otherwise stagnant group of individuals.

> 66We realized that our largest asset was our work force and that our growth would come from asset appreciation.99
>
> LARRY COLIN
> President,
> Colin Service Systems

Once a month, any employee of Chef Allen's restaurant in Miami can go out to dinner at another restaurant with a friend or spouse, and owner Allen Susser will kick in up to $50. The only condition is that the employee must write a one-page report detailing various aspects of the experience, such as service, ambiance, and food preparation, and give an oral report before the entire staff. In this way, employees learn how other restaurants serve *their* customers.

To help give workers an idea of the cost of "disposable" hotel stock such as pens, shampoo, and copy paper, John Giattino, general manager of Clarion Hotel in Virginia Beach, Virginia, stages a monthly game of "The Price Is Right" with various hotel departments. The price of each item is written on cards that are placed face down on a table along with the items themselves, and employees try to guess the price of each item. Winners receive prizes, including cash and tickets to local amusement parks. In playing the game, employees also learn a valuable lesson about the importance of not wasting company resources.

————

A t Midlothian, Texas's Chaparral Steel, approximately 85 percent of the company's employees are in the process of taking one or more of 22 different courses offered by the company. Security guards are trained to act as paramedics and accounting clerks, and other employees are encouraged to learn every job in their departments. Not only are employees paid $20 for each four-hour training session that they attend on their own time, their pay increases as they complete more courses. Chaparral Steel ends up with more versatile and valuable employees, and the employees are energized by the opportunity to broaden the tasks and assignments they perform on the job.

————

Q uill Corporation of Lincolnshire, Illinois, sponsors an annual Career Development Week for its employees. A college fair is conducted on-site, giving employees a chance to talk to representatives of local schools and

SUGGESTION BOX

☞ Allow employees to select and attend the training course of their choice.

☞ Encourage employees to work on an advanced degree.

☞ Before they attend a course, take the time to meet with employees to discuss what you hope they will learn from it. After they attend a course, take the time to meet with them to see what they learned and how they will apply their new knowledge.

☞ Have employees share what they learned at a seminar with the rest of the group.

"Above all, IBM's Thomas Watson trained, and trained, and trained."

PETER DRUCKER
Management Guru

arrange to take courses, the tuition for which is reimbursed by the company. Quill benefits from better educated employees and the employees are excited by the opportunity to work toward their college degrees.

———

At Diversified Expositions, a trade show production company in Portland, Maine, every employee attends quarterly job-related learning sessions presented by an outside consultant. Topics, which are chosen by the employees themselves, have included: constructive feedback, listening skills, and empowerment. As a result of these sessions, employees developed their own performance evaluation system.

———

Rosenbluth International, a travel agency headquartered in Philadelphia, sponsors monthly seminar programs for enriching both personal and professional life for its employees. Topics range from handling difficult situations and goal-setting, to food, fitness, and recycling. The "Live the Spirit" program presents a new topic every month and employees nationwide can benefit.

———

Sausage maker Johnsonville Foods of Sheboygan Falls, Wisconsin, encourages every employee to spend one day a year observing another employee perform his or her job. Employees learn something new about their co-workers, and about other departments within the company.

———

At Palo Alto, California, public relations firm Cunningham Communications, *all* employees—including secretaries and other support staff—are encouraged to read at least one hour a day during working hours, from trade journals, newspapers, business magazines, or anything else connected with public relations.

———

At the industrial controls group of Milwaukee auto parts manufacturer Allen-Bradley, employees choose three work-related topics each year to explore in depth. Each topic then becomes the focus of four months of intensive training and learning.

———

Learning about all aspects of a company energizes all levels of company management. At Physio-Control, a cardiac-care equipment maker in Redmond, Washington, it's standard operating procedure for senior managers to spend a week on the assembly line learning how the company's products are manufactured. According to technical support supervisor Tom Clemson, "It's not uncommon to see the vice president down on the production floor soldering parts together."

———

To help give employees an appreciation of how the company spends its money, CEO Terry Fulwiler of Wisconsin Label, a specialty printer in Algoma, Wisconsin, printed playing cards with financial terms such as *labor* and *depreciation* and handed out cards to all com-

Five Keys to Growth

A report issued by the Center for Creative Leadership in Greensboro, North Carolina, cited five key experiences that help employees develop and grow:

1. Challenging jobs.

2. Interacting with other people, mostly bosses.

3. Hardships.

4. Coursework.

5. Off-the-job experiences.

❝Always assume each and every person wants to do a better job and grow.❞

STEVE FARRAR
Senior Vice President,
Wendy's International

pany employees. Next he printed play money amounting to $2 million and invited the employees to a meeting. At the beginning of the meeting, Fulwiler piled the $2 millon in a stack and then invited the holders of each card to come forward and "claim" their share of the company's revenues. After everyone had taken his or her piece, what was left was the company's profit. Says Fulwiler, "The meeting ran for an hour and a half. People had no idea how much money was spent each month on certain items." Now they do.

———

After taking a course in statistical process control, Wilma Porter, an employee at General Electric's mobile communications plant in Lynchburg, Virginia, applied what she had learned to her job. Over the course of just 12 weeks, she saved the company $100,000 by salvaging parts that were routinely thrown out. Not only did GE's bottom line improve as a result of Porter's efforts, but she was energized and empowered by having the freedom to apply what she had learned at school to her work.

———

After working a 40-hour shift, employees at Quad/Graphics, a magazine printer in Pewaukee, Wisconsin, are offered a voluntary day of training in areas that relate either to work or life. The classes are usually taught in-house and are frequently full.

———

Sometimes it's necessary to step outside of one's normal role in an organization to learn something new. At Beth Israel Hospital in Boston, doctors occasionally dress as maintenance staff and roam the hospital halls. Why? To learn how it feels to be treated as "support staff" and to find ways of improving the hospital environment.

———

During a quarterly meeting at one of the Dayton, Ohio-based Iams Company plants, the company's president challenged all employees to learn the company's four key business goals, and announced that there would be a "quiz" at the next quarterly meeting. To make "studying" easier, the pet food maker distributed T-shirts with the four goals printed on the front to all 150 employees. Every day, somebody in the plant was bound to be wearing one of the T-shirts, and reminding everyone of the goals. The challenge energized the workforce at the same time that it drove the company's message home. At the next meeting, everyone passed the quiz.

———

At Viking Freight System, a trucking firm located in San Jose, California, sales representatives set aside at least one day a month to ride along with company truck drivers to get a perspective of the company from the frontline. The trips benefit the sales staff because they develop a closer rapport with drivers, and the

> ❝I think business increasingly recognizes that having a workforce that is trained, that is educated, that has the right skills is important to maintaining the great competitive steps we've made in the last few years.❞
>
> STEVEN RATTNER
> Managing Director,
> Lazard Freres & Co.

❝Well-trained and dedicated employees are the only sustainable source of competitive strength.❞

ROBERT REICH
Former U.S. Secretary
of Labor

drivers, because they learn how to sell the company's services to customers.

———

To learn firsthand about the problems cashiers were having with a new cash register system, managers at Wegmans, a supermarket chain headquartered in Rochester, New York, worked a four-hour shift in place of the regular cashiers.

———

National Semiconductor in Santa Clara, California, hired a professional artist to render the company's vision statement as a four-color drawing. The drawing depicts the corporate spaceship zooming over a chasm of industrial uncertainty, carried on the winds of customer delight, innovation, and quality. Although management commissioned the original drawing, *all* employees participate in updating it.

———

After employees at Linda L. Miles & Associates, a dental practices consulting and training firm in Virginia Beach, Virginia, return from seminars, they report on the three most important things they learned at departmental meetings. Says CEO Linda Miles, "After our shipping clerk went to a postal service seminar, all 20 of our employees learned how complex this job was and were more cooperative when we made changes in our mailroom."

———

Alfred P. Sloan, the man who during the 1920s and '30s built General Motors into the world's top manufacturing company, used to disappear from Detroit for a week every three months. During that week, he would work as a salesman or assistant service manager in General Motors dealerships in three different cities. Upon his return to Detroit Sloan would quickly write and distribute memos to his staff on market and style trends, changing customer preferences and behavior, and dealer service issues.

Clay Page, CEO of Co-op Building Consultants in Corpus Christi, Texas, farms out the task of reading trade magazines to his workers. Carpenters read stories about the newest saws and framers study articles about the advantages and disadvantages of aluminum versus wooden two-by-fours. If a worker thinks an article is worthwhile, he clips it and sends it to Page for his review.

The manufacture of steel is a hot and dirty job. However, at Chaparral Steel of Midlothian, Texas, steel workers are given the opportunity to get out of the plant and join the company's sales people on customer calls. According to Brad Cowan, a melt-shop operator who traveled to Mexico, Los Angeles, and San Diego with two salespeople, "It was interesting to see where your stuff ends up. I got to talk with the people who run the companies and tell them that if they had complaints they should let us know."

Energizing Values

Here are Perot Systems' corporate values:

- We serve our clients with innovative, responsive solutions to their needs.

- We treasure our people by attracting, developing, and recognizing outstanding people, and caring for them and their families.

- We operate with integrity by treating our clients, people, and suppliers in a fair and honest manner—as we want to be treated.

- We reward our stakeholders by producing strong financial performance from which everyone benefits.

- We contribute to our communities by using our talents and resources to better the conditions in the diverse communities in which we work.

66Not only must
workers learn and be
motivated to do so,
managers must learn
as well. Indeed,
workers teaching
their peers has value;
nobody knows the
details of a job as
well as those doing
it, and workers
often best perceive
the problems in a job.
However, if workers
cannot inform man-
agers—and managers
cannot learn and
respond—workers'
insights have no
credibility, and the
notion of their part-
nership with manage-
ment becomes empty
verbiage.99

DR. MITCHELL RABKIN
President, Beth Israel
Hospital, Boston

New employees at Phelps County Bank in Rolla, Missouri, are given a chart titled, "How We Make Each Dollar and How It Is Spent." Company president Emma Lou Brent walks the new employees through the chart as a part of their orientation—pointing out important figures along the way. Employees are more involved when they know their part in how the bank makes money and what they can do to help.

———

Tassani Communications, an advertising agency in Chicago, sponsors "Food for Thought" brown-bag lunches where employees learn about a wide variety of topics—both job- and non-job-related. Lecture topics have included stress management, crime prevention, and time management.

———

At Second Wind, an athletic-shoe-care product manufacturer in Paso Robles, California, all employees are trained to take orders for the company's products in case the sales staff is out to lunch or busy with other calls. Non-sales employees are energized by the opportunity to serve customers directly.

———

Employees can be energized by the opportunity to explain what they do on the job to their co-workers. Integrated Genetics, a bio-engineering company in Framingham, Massachusetts, brings its employees closer together by sponsoring a weekly in-house seminar titled

"Science for Non-Scientists," in which company scientists explain their work to the company's administrative staff.

———

To keep up with the latest business books, employees at Davis, Hays & Co., a public-relations firm in Hackensack, New Jersey, present book reports to one another during working hours. Employees are allowed to choose the books they want to read and the company pays for them. Besides keeping employees up to date, it gives them an opportunity to work on their oral presentation skills.

———

Employees can easily lose interest in their jobs when they are given little or no training. At Paychex, a payroll and business services firm headquartered in Rochester, New York, every new salesperson goes through seven weeks of training before he or she is allowed to meet with prospects. As a result, new-hires earn more than their draw twice as quickly as before they implemented the training, and staff turnover has fallen dramatically.

———

SUGGESTION BOX

☞ Ask your employees to make lists of opportunities for career development, such as taking on new assignments, developing new skills, and participating in cross-functional teams. Then, meet with them to determine how these opportunities can be arranged.

☞ Create individual career development plans for each employee, detailing the skills they would like to learn and opportunities available for them, including potential next jobs.

☞ Discuss career development as part of every annual performance review.

Interesting, Challenging Work

F ace it—if your employees are stuck doing the same tasks over and over again, they're going to find themselves in a rut. However, new challenges can reenergize them and restore their enthusiasm. Remember how you felt when you first started in your job—the excitement and anticipation, and occasional nervousness about starting something new? Well, you can help your employees retain or recapture that feeling by allowing them to take on interesting new challenges.

> **"If you want someone to do a good job, give them a good job to do."**
>
> FREDERICK HERZBERG
> Management Theorist

According to a study conducted by the Greensboro, North Carolina-based Center for Creative Leadership, a non-profit institution that does research and training on the topic of leadership, there are five ways to create new challenges for your employees without assigning them to entirely new jobs. Although the Center's study focused on creating new challenges as a way of developing managers, the results can also be used to rekindle employee interest and energy in their jobs.

1 Assign small projects and start-ups which require learning new tasks, working under time pressure, and dealing with new groups of people. Such assignments might include:

■ Creating a task force on a pressing business problem.

- Planning an off-site meeting, conference, or convention.

- Handling a negotiation with a customer.

- Installing a new system.

- Working with a plant shut-down crew.

- Integrating systems across units.

- Supervising product, program, equipment, or systems purchases.

- Supervising the liquidation of a product, program, equipment, or system.

- Presenting a proposal to top management.

- Going off-site to deal with a dissatisfied customer.

- Going to a campus as a recruiter.

- Supervising a study team.

- Organizing a company picnic.

- Going on a business trip to a foreign country.

- Supervising the furnishing of offices.

- Supervising the assigning of office space.

- Making speeches for the organization.

- Writing press releases.

- Serving at a trade-show booth.

- Working with the credit union board or committee.

- Serving on a new project/product review committee.

SUGGESTION BOX

☞ *Every employee needs some part of his or her job to be highly interesting. Find out what part of your employees' jobs are the most motivating to them and try to assign work accordingly.*

☞ *When hiring new employees, find out what work tasks they like to do the most.*

☞ *For veteran employees, continue to find ways to keep their jobs interesting through new assignments and challenges.*

❝Work can provide the opportunity for spiritual and personal, as well as financial, growth. If it doesn't, then we're wasting far too much of our lives on it.❞

JAMES A. AUTRY
Love and Profit—The Art of Caring Leadership

- Working short periods in other units.

- Managing a renovation project.

- Launching a new product or program.

- Following a new product or system through its entire cycle.

- Working on a project with a tight deadline.

- Managing the visit of a VIP.

2 Assign small-scope jumps and fix-its which emphasize team building, individual responsibility, dealing with the boss, encouraging subordinates, and managing time pressure. Examples include:

- Creating a symbol or rallying cry for change and implementation.

- Managing an ad hoc group of inexperienced people.

- Managing an ad hoc group to help energize a static operation.

- Managing an ad hoc group in a rapidly expanding operation.

- Dealing with a business crisis.

- Working on an "undoable" project, one where the last person who tried it failed.

- Supervising outplacement.

- Supervising cost cutting.

- Designing new, simpler effectiveness measures.

- Working on something the person hates to do.

- Resolving conflict among warring subordinates.

3 Make small strategic assignments which emphasize presentation and analysis skills. The following assignments will fulfill this need:

- Summarizing a new trend or technique and presenting it to others.

- Writing a proposal for a new system or product.

- Spending a week with customers and writing a report.

- Doing a competitive analysis.

- Writing a speech for someone higher in the organization.

- Writing up a policy statement.

- Studying customer needs.

- Holding a postmortem on a failed project.

- Doing a problem-prevention analysis.

- Studying innovations by customers and/or competitors.

- Interviewing outsiders on their view of the organization.

- Evaluating the impact of training.

- Writing up a contingency scenario.

> **"People want to be challenged. Money isn't everything. I want to create a culture where people look forward to coming to work in the morning and feel good at night when they leave."**
>
> BOB CANTWELL
> President,
> Hadady Corporation

**❝The art of govern-
ing consists of not
allowing men to grow
old in their jobs.❞**

NAPOLEON BONAPARTE

4 Have your employees do coursework and/or take on coaching assignments that require learning something new and are intellectually challenging, both of which can lead to heightened self-awareness. Some ways of doing this include:

■ Teaching a course or workshop.

■ Teaching someone how to do something new.

■ Designing a training course.

■ Doing a self-study project.

■ Attending a self-awareness course.

■ Training as an assessor in an assessment center.

■ Studying a new technical area.

5 Have your employees undertake activities away from work that emphasize individual leadership skills, working with new people, and learning to influence and persuade. The following activities are good for starters:

■ Becoming active in a professional organization.

■ Joining a community board.

■ Becoming active in a volunteer organization.

■ Acting as a consultant on a problem or issue outside of the job.

■ Coaching children's sports.

PART II

ENERGIZING TEAMS

There is a fundamental shift in the way organizations are getting work done today. Most companies are trying to make greater use of teamwork through ad hoc teams, cross-functional teams, self-directed work teams, and so on. For many companies, teams are being used to compensate for the massive downsizing that has occurred in the last decade—especially in the ranks of middle management. For other companies, the use of teams simply represents a more efficient way of handling complex tasks. As the saying goes, "None of us is as smart as all of us."

While business leaders have talked about the importance of teamwork for years, in many organizations only recently have the teams actually been empowered to make decisions independently of management. Today's teams are expected to decide what needs to be done and then find a way to do it. Participating in this process is more complicated than working alone since you cannot unilaterally decide what to do and how to do it when you are working with others. The work usually takes longer than expected, and obtaining the agreement of all team members can be painstaking and difficult. Add to that the amount of wasted time that often occurs within teams, and it is little wonder that for many the team experience can be so frustrating.

But often the positives outweigh the negatives. Employees who participate on teams may become energized by the experience of working together with their co-workers to find ways to improve company systems and processes, solve problems, or plan for opportunities. If the team is successful in achieving its goals, the experience is usually a very satisfying one and leads to a strong identification with and pride in the team and its accomplishments.

This section examines how companies today are energizing employees through the use of teams and the team process. Topics covered range from determining how a team is oriented and how it defines its purpose, to the mechanics of running effective meetings, to establishing a team accountability system that really works.

A Clear Purpose and Well-Defined Goals

When teams are empowered, they are naturally energizing to employees because they allow them to have a measure of control and influence over their work. However, energized teams don't just happen, they must be developed. To function effectively and efficiently—and to keep members at a high level of energy—every team needs to have a clear purpose, as well as established goals and rules. Every member of the team needs to know the team's goals, his or her place in the team, as well as the team's operating principles. When these boundaries aren't spelled out clearly and routinely reinforced, the team loses energy and momentum.

Boston-based Beth Israel Hospital's PREPARE/21 program, established to cut costs and improve service, has dramatically increased the level of its employees' energy by encouraging their involvement and creativity. Under PREPARE/21—Participation, Responsibility, Education, Productivity, Accountability, Recognition, and Excellence for the 21st Century—employees organize teams that study ways to cut costs and improve the organization. Beth Israel goes a step further by allowing employees to share in the savings that accrue as a result of team suggestions. In the first year of the

> **"**Most people want to be part of a team.**"**
>
> CANDACE KASPERS
> President,
> Kaspers & Associates

SUGGESTION BOX

☞ *Create a mission statement for the team. This will define your purpose and set boundaries for the scope of the team's work.*

☞ *Make sure that the team develops specific goals, and that it periodically revisits and updates them.*

☞ *Post the team's purpose and rules for operation at each meeting.*

program, employees split $1 million—half of the $2 million the hospital saved as a result of their suggestions.

———

Teams that are empowered to achieve results quickly and independently are energizing to the employees who participate in them. Cambridge Technology Partners, a software development firm in Cambridge, Massachusetts, is noted for taking on and successfully completing time-critical projects for corporate giants such as Microsoft and AT&T. The company relies on teams of energized employees to achieve its project goals. Project manager Tammy Urban has defined four rules for fast teams:

■ **Let the group make its own rules.** If a team is going to be 100 percent committed to completing a project on time and within budget—regardless of the personal sacrifice involved—the members of the team have to be in charge of their own destiny. "You want to make sure people have a say in how they're going to work together," says Urban.

■ **Speak up early and often.** When a team member runs into a problem, the sooner he or she gets help with it, the less likely the problem will get out of control and threaten the project. Urban's teams have a rule that if a problem can't be solved in two minutes or less, the members should ask for help.

■ **Learn as you go.** During the course of a large project for AT&T, Urban conducted half-day review sessions at the end of each phase of

the project. These reviews, which involved team members and other company staff, benefited not only the project, but the entire organization. According to Urban, "We'd take what we'd learned, what had worked well, what we wanted to improve, and deliver that to the rest of the organization. That way other staffers learned from our experience."

▪ **Fast has to be fun.** People can burn out quickly when the pressure's on and no one is having any fun. The AT&T project team planned weekly outings to reenergize staff: "We'd play darts, shoot pool," Urban says, adding "Teams work best when you get to know each other outside of work—what people's interests are, who they are. Personal connections go a long way when you're developing complex software on a tight schedule."

Some companies have been energizing their employees for decades. Long before quality circles and total quality management became the rage in American business, McCormick & Company, a spice-maker located in Hunt Valley, Maryland, established multiple management boards. These serve as sort of a junior board of directors and are made up of middle managers from throughout the company. With 12 boards in place, members have the opportunity to work on solutions to company problems and to review and consider new ideas. For example, one multiple management board took up a review of coupon redemption houses, and found that the company could save money by moving its

66Make it clear that everyone is on the same team. Avoid practices that imply that some . . . are on the first team and others are part of another.**99**

Paul S. George
Professor, University of
Florida, Gainesville

account to a different house. McCormick used this information as leverage in getting its current redemption house to lower its price.

————

It often takes several different programs working together to energize an entire workforce. At Honda of America Manufacturing based in Marysville, Ohio, the Voluntary Involvement Program, or VIP, consists of four parts:

1. New Honda-Circles (groups of five to ten associates who meet together to suggest improvements or solve problems)

2. A suggestion program

3. Quality awards

4. Safety awards

Unlike elsewhere, however, at Honda employees implement their own suggestions. When a group of associates suggested that Honda allow employees to buy stock at a discount through payroll deduction, manager Don English teamed them up with other associates and the company's legal staff. The team did extensive research on the issue. When it was complete, Honda implemented the group's recommendations.

————

When employees are energized, they will often develop their own rules of team conduct, as they did at Viscosity Oil in Willowbrook, Illinois. The customer service team established a code of conduct, signed by the members of the team and posted for all to see:

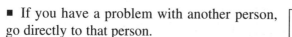

- If you have a problem with another person, go directly to that person.

- Don't put your finger in anyone else's face.

- No back-stabbing—don't say negative things about anyone.

- If someone comes to you with a problem, don't share it with others.

- Come to work with a smile and keep it!

At Nissan Motor Manufacturing in Smyrna, Tennessee, Japanese methods of employee involvement and teamwork are an integral part of creating and maintaining employee energy. Involvement Through Teamwork (ITT) teams, consisting of technicians, engineers, and managers, meet weekly to discuss and develop solutions for production problems on the assembly line. In the Involvement Circles program, groups of technicians pick a project to tackle from a list of suggestions. Involvement Circles have developed 225 new ideas that have been implemented at the plant, including the installation of robots and other innovations.

Creating opportunities for young employees to interact directly with an organization's top management can be very energizing—for both the employees and the managers. German computer superpower Siemens Nixdorf Information Systems, located in Paderborn, formed a team of 23 young, talented employees—all age

Leadership Builders

In their book, *The Wisdom of Teams*, Jon R. Katzenbach and Douglas K. Smith suggest that six things are necessary for good team leadership:

1. Keep the purpose, goals, and approach relevant and meaningful.

2. Build commitment and confidence.

3. Strengthen the mix and level of skills.

4. Manage relationships with outsiders, including removing obstacles.

5. Create opportunities for others.

6. Do real work.

> **"When you're hiring, you want people who love you and love the values of your company. You don't want confrontation all the time. Also you don't want people who only have a sense of their own growth, not that of others, or of the company's."**
>
> ANITA RODDICK
> Group Managing Director,
> The Body Shop

40 or under—to advise the company's management board on the breakthrough technologies, competitive forces, and demographic trends that will likely affect business in the year 2005. Team member Stacy Welsh says, "Our role is to challenge the board. They look to us for perspective."

At General Motors's Cadillac engine plant in Livonia, Michigan, productivity and quality improved after all employees were assigned to groups of eight to fifteen people called "business teams," which meet at least once a week and energize employees in the following ways:

■ They are highly autonomous—with responsibility for their own scheduling, training, problem solving, and other activities.

■ They develop their own quantitative performance indicators.

■ They employ a pay-for-knowledge system (employees are paid more if they learn more) to encourage employees to learn *all* plant jobs.

■ Awards for suggestions are given to teams as a whole, encouraging people to work together.

■ Performance appraisals emphasize support for the business team.

■ With only one job category—quality operator—job specialization is virtually eliminated.

For teams to be energized, they must be given responsibility and authority. Vice president

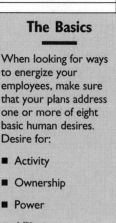

Robert Hershock and corporate scientist David J. Braun of 3M (Minnesota Mining & Manufacturing), headquartered in St. Paul, reviewed the work of an action team that had developed a new model of respirator in record time, and discovered five keys to team success:

1. Empower the team. According to Hershock, this means "giving the team the authority to make decisions and then act on them."

2. Let the teams manage risk. In other words, they should be able to select the amount of risk that offers the highest likelihood of success.

3. Let the team control the budget. Teams must make all decisions on project matters including financial ones.

4. Recognize the phases the team progresses through. Some phases of a project are smoother than others. Be alert to signs that the team needs additional management support or coaching at critical times in the project life cycle.

5. Let the team be involved in the reward process. After all, who knows better what motivates the team than its members?

Fireman's Fund Insurance Company's personal insurance division in Novato, California, divided its employees into work units organized around its customers. Several levels of management were cut, and whenever possible individuals were assigned whole jobs instead of fragmented work tasks. With these changes, employees felt

The Basics

When looking for ways to energize your employees, make sure that your plans address one or more of eight basic human desires. Desire for:

- Activity
- Ownership
- Power
- Affiliation
- Competence
- Achievement
- Recognition
- Meaning

they had a real stake in making customers happy, efficiency increased by 35 to 40 percent, systems investments declined by $5 million a year, and endorsement turnaround was cut from 21 *days* to 24 to 48 *hours*.

———

Many teams are energized by having a voice in their own membership. Before an applicant can be hired at Whole Foods, a natural foods grocery chain headquartered in Austin, Texas, he or she has to first be recommended for a job on a specific team by the store leader and then voted in by at least two-thirds of the team members.

———

> **❝To really feel included in the corporate culture, workers should know why the company exists, its basic values, and the ways in which it cares for its customers.❞**
>
> RICHARD ROSS
> President,
> Tri Companies

Team Spirit

It takes more to create a team than designating team members and giving them an assignment. Successful teams are infused with an energizing spirit that draws the participants together into a cohesive unit and has everyone pulling together to reach a common goal. There are many ways to help instill a sense of teamwork in a team, including group challenges, team-building exercises, and the promotion of team culture. The ultimate result is an organization where the whole truly adds up to more than the sum of its parts.

Whenever a new Woburn, Massachusetts-based Bertucci's restaurant opens, CEO Joe Crungale and his top managers energize the restaurant's dishwashers, waiters, and bartenders by working side by side with them for the first two weeks of operation. According to Crungale, "We know they need help, so we just fill in wherever we can."

> **❝The ratio of 'We's' to 'I's' is the best indicator of the development of a team.❞**
>
> LEWIS D. EIGEN
> Executive Vice President,
> University Research Corp.

Management at Lyondell Petrochemical in Houston has implemented an impressive array of teams to involve workers in decision making and keep them energized. Teams tackle quality improvement, problem solving, quality breakthrough, and multifunctional business issues. Vice president Debbie Starnes says, "Teamwork is very important here. Trying to be a Lone Ranger and make yourself look good at the

"Nothing, not even the most advanced technology, is as formidable as people working together enthusiastically toward a shared goal. Whether as an army, a nation, or a corporation—people become unstoppable when they are moved by a common vision, and have the power and tools to achieve it.**"**

United Technologies
Corporation brochure

expense of everybody else or at the risk of not getting a job done, just doesn't work here."

To help build teamwork among employees, management at Collins and Aikman Textile Group in Dalton, Georgia, sent employees to a special empowerment training program. At this program, employees undertook a series of outdoor exercises such as scaling a 42-foot-tall wall. Teammates on the ground held safety ropes for their counterparts on the wall, and directed the climbers on where to place their hands and feet. Energized by programs such as this, employees submitted more than 1,800 suggestions over a two-year period, 75 percent of which were adopted by management.

At clothing retailer Katherine Barchetti's shops, in Pittsburgh, Pennsylvania, sales associates work in informal, ad hoc teams. As one associate greets a customer, another looks up his or her record in the store's computer database while still another pulls merchandise from hangers and shelves and brings it to the customer.

At Rosenbluth International, the Philadelphia-based corporate travel agency, the ability for prospective employees to fit into the company's team culture is so important that managers will go out of their way to hire someone who may not have all the skills needed for the position, but who has the right *attitude*. According to president and CEO Hal Rosenbluth, "That is rule number one for us." Rosenbluth invites prospects to join him in a game of basketball or on a business trip. On one occasion, an otherwise promising candidate was shown the door after he blamed his teammates for the loss of a basketball game. But when a candidate with the right attitude failed the typing test, the company encouraged her to practice and return in two weeks for another test. She did, and she got the job.

———

Instead of asking applicants about their skills in working a balance sheet or designing an electrical circuit, interviewers at electronics manufacturer Hewlett-Packard in Palo Alto, California, are much more likely to ask a question that indicates the candidates' teamwork skills, such as "Describe in detail an experience you had working in an intense, long-lasting small group."

———

Susan Van Weelden, associate dean at McHenry County College's Center for Commerce and Economic Development in Crystal Lake, Illinois, always includes her secretary as a member of "the team." Van Weelden's secretary is energized by the opportunity to participate in higher-level decision making, and the rest of the team is energized by her unique perspective on the organization.

———

Time-Tested Energizers

Here are some time-tested ways to energize employees:

■ Take employees from different levels and areas to lunch and ask what they would change in the organization and how they'd change it.

■ Communicate all information to all employees all of the time.

■ Encourage employees to improve one process, procedure, or aspect of their job every day.

■ Encourage employees to set time aside each day to focus uninterrupted on their highest-priority tasks.

■ Send a problem out to all employees and ask for their suggestions on how to solve it.

■ Give employees permission to say "yes" to customers and the resources to do so.

■ Break down barriers between departments.

■ Encourage employees to take chances and let them know that it's okay to fail in the process.

Rules to Live By

Perot System's codes of behavior—aka "work styles"—set the stage for an energized workplace:

■ Lead by example.

■ Conduct our personal and professional life in a manner that will bring credit to ourselves, our family, and our company at all times.

■ Operate in the center of the field of ethical behavior—never on the sidelines.

■ Create and maintain an atmosphere of mutual trust and respect.

■ Listen to people and be open to new ideas.

■ Encourage every team member to take risks, exercise initiative, deliver quality results, and never be afraid to make mistakes.

■ Create a supportive environment that nurtures personal and professional growth.

■ Do what we say we are going to do—and even more.

■ And finally, while we are building a great company . . . have fun!

Managers can energize employees by communicating their personal vision of what teamwork means to them. Nancy Singer, president and CEO of the Retail Credit Services Division of First of America Bank Corporation based in Kalamazoo, Michigan, bought colorful computer mouse pads and note cubes inscribed with the word *teamwork* and handed them out to all attendees at a recent planning meeting. Singer has taken the extra step of developing a *teamwork* acronym, which appears on all memos and other internal correspondence:

Together
Everyone
Achieves
More
With
Organization
Recognition and
Knowledge

———

To promote teamwork, employees at Norman Howe & Associates, a marketing and consulting firm in Pasadena, California, make lists of their tasks or projects every Monday morning. The lists are shared with supervisors and read out loud to employees at a one-hour staff lunch. Co-workers often suggest new ways to approach tasks or offer to help each other out.

———

Teams of custodians at Texas A&M University in College Station hold an annual "Olympics" designed to test their proficiency with everything from dust mops to floor waxers. Just as in the real Olympics, the participants hold preliminary meets in such key events as the "Peanut Push" and the "Obstacle Course." Staff build important teamwork skills through their pre-Olympic preparations, and have fun too.

———

One advantage for employees at Microsoft in Redmond, Washington, is that there are many avenues for employees to pursue success. One way Microsoft's management promotes this is by encouraging employees to form work teams to tackle critical product issues. "There is very little dead wood here. People care passionately about what they're doing," says one employee. "I think that's because we've done a pretty good job of organizing small teams and empowering those teams. Employees feel like they own the product. There's a world of difference from the more hierarchical organizations where decisions are filtered down from the top."

———

At Honda of America Manufacturing in Marysville, Ohio, executives make a major effort to mitigate worker fear of management, which can stifle initiative, and to create team cohesiveness. This effort pays huge dividends in improved communication and company effectiveness. Says production associate Johnna Haughn, "Other places I worked, I was afraid of my bosses. But at Honda, it's all teamwork. Management will dig right in there with you to

> **"Involving people in the business is the most effective way to produce an organization in which people know more, care more, and do the right things."**
>
> EDWARD LAWLER III
> Professor, University of Southern California

> **"**Think about what kind of planning environment supports teamwork. Individual spaces will be smaller. There will be more dedicated team rooms, more group spaces.**"**
>
> MICHAEL JOROFF
> Director of Research,
> MIT School of
> Architecture

help solve problems. They don't just stand back and tell you what to do."

———

Teams of energized workers, not managers, set the agenda at Xerox's annual Teamwork Day. Attended by thousands of employees at several major Xerox facilities, including the company's headquarters in Stamford, Connecticut, and broadcast to other Xerox offices worldwide via satellite, Teamwork Day is an opportunity for Xerox employee quality teams to get their stories out to their co-workers. Recent teams diverted 6,500 tons of waste from a landfill through their recycling program and introduced an exercise program that reduced on-the-job injuries by 71 percent.

———

At Boston Market, a restaurant chain headquartered in Denver, managers at all levels of the organization work on team projects together via on-line computer links. Together these energized project teams change menus, solve distribution problems, resolve customer complaints, and plan company expansions.

———

Employees at Vitalink Pharmacy Services, based in Naperville, Illinois, pulled together teams of frontline employees from across the country to develop job-specific training and orientation guides for new employees; best operating practices and policies; and a quality management process to monitor and manage change while ensuring consistency of service delivery to all customers. Employees were energized by participating in teams with their counterparts from other parts of the country.

———

Much of Chrysler's recent success can be attributed to the company's use of employee teams to kick off new projects. When the Auburn Hills, Michigan-based company is going to create a new model automobile, or update an old one, Chrysler forms a multidisciplinary team of 700 or so employees from throughout the organization, including representatives from finance, marketing, engineering, and design. The team and Chrysler management agree to a set of objectives, and then the team is allowed to follow its own path to meeting them—energizing the members of the team in the process. This approach has resulted in the hot-selling Ram pickup truck, the Neon subcompact, and the Viper sports car.

———

At Motor Cargo, a trucking firm in Salt Lake City, Utah, a team of truckers worked together to produce, direct, and perform in a video on how to catch billing errors. Not only did this team effort energize the participants, but the company saved an estimated $16.48 per bill, and employees loved it. Says employee involvement coordinator Kevin Avery, "It's the first training video I've seen people actually excited to watch."

———

> **"I prefer things that are spontaneous. Things I hate the most are the routine, accepted things like an annual company picnic. I think it's important for there to be an element of humor, laughter. It adds to the company. It's one more thing that makes you want to get up in the morning and go to work."**
>
> JOEL SLUTZKY
> Chairman,
> Odetics, Inc.

Three Simple Principles

Whole Foods, the Austin, Texas-based natural foods grocer, has established three principles to ensure employee involvement *and* high productivity:

1. All work is teamwork.

2. Anything worth doing is worth measuring.

3. Be your own toughest competitor.

Whenever there is a problem with an order at Jagemann Stamping, a tool-and-die shop in Manitowoc, Wisconsin, a small team of line workers is sent to investigate and come up with solutions. "Their involvement helps raise their level of commitment to the customer because they see how the product is used and have a sense of the conditions that the customer has to deal with," says vice-chairman Bob Jagemann. Employees are also energized by the opportunity to work together and to meet with customers to solve their problems.

———

To help energize veteran employees when new-hires are introduced to the company, Terri and Steve Cowan, owners of Professional Salon Concepts, a supplier of hair-care products and services in Joliet, Illinois, set up a system of team interviews. The company's fifteen salespeople and five department heads are divided into five teams. Starting at 5:00 P.M., job candidates are interviewed for 20 minutes by each team and rated against a list of 20 to 25 attributes considered necessary by the company. After the interviews are complete, the teams vote, the results are tallied, and the highest-ranking candidates are invited back for an interview with the Cowans. Not only are the company's employees more enthusiastic about the new-hires but, since the teams have a vested interest in the success of their recommended candidates, the training of new employees is much less of a problem than before.

———

At Delta Airlines, headquartered in Atlanta, when someone recognizes that a team of employees has gone above and beyond, that person fills out a Team Recognition Card and presents it to the team. A copy of the comments explaining how the team went above and beyond is given to each team member's supervisor and then the team card is entered into a drawing. Each team card drawn is awarded $500 to be donated to the charity or civic organization of the team's choice. It's just another way of showing that Delta people work together to go above and beyond for each other, their customers . . . and their communities!

> **"**Everybody has noted the astonishing sources of energy that seem available to those who enjoy what they are doing or find meaning in what they are doing.**"**
>
> CHARLES GARFIELD
> President, Performance Sciences Corp.

———

Randy Dorr, a former supervisor at MCI, tells the story of how he energized a team of telemarketers: "Our group was the worst-performing sales group at the time. I nicknamed it the "F-Troop" and told my manager that I'd make them the best-performing group in three months. He thought I was crazy. On the spur of the moment I told the group that if they got to be No. 1, I'd call their mothers and tell them how great they were. And as individuals met their performance goals, I did just that. The employees always came to work the next day feeling like a champion. And we reached our goal of becoming No. 1 in the company."

———

Productive Meetings

In meetings, teams get together to decide how they will approach and handle opportunities and problems. Meetings bring together employees from throughout an organization to discuss and deal with issues of common interest. Sometimes simply being invited to attend and contribute is energizing to employees. Unfortunately, much of the time workers spend in meetings is wasted—participants come unprepared, there are no clear goals or agendas, or some employees dominate the sessions while others retreat into the woodwork. In fact, it's estimated that approximately 53 percent of all meeting time is wasted for various reasons. This said, when the goals are clear and when everyone has a chance to participate, meetings can be a golden opportunity to energize employees.

66Meetings of cross-functional teams of employees are clearly the most effective way to include employees from all levels and all parts of an organization in the decision-making process.99

PETER ECONOMY
Business Consultant

Solar Communications, in Naperville, Illinois, closed down its printing operations for a day and brought all 320 full-time workers to a local community college for an all-day brainstorming retreat. After energizing speeches and introductions by top management, the group broke into departmental groups to discuss staffing problems, production bottlenecks, and other issues. The result was a list of 50 key problem areas to be addressed by an employee task force.

Every other month, the president of T.L.C. Child Care Centers in Green Bay, Wisconsin, takes her employee team out for a formal "gripe" session over pizza. During the first hour, the floor is open for criticism of anything and anybody—including management. During the second hour, employees discuss solutions to the problems they raised in the first hour.

———

At Tinderbox International, a tobacco and gift store franchise based in Los Angeles, the Committee of 90—a team of the franchise's top performers—meets quarterly with less successful franchisees to provide advice and support. These meetings energize both the members of the Committee—who enjoy the opportunity to share their expertise—and the franchisees, whose operations improve as a result of the experience.

———

At SynOptics Communications, in Mountain View, California, the company holds a quarterly lunch in the headquarters building for the key people of two divisions. They are seated at five tables and each is assigned a problem to solve. After lunch each table presents its solutions to the rest of the group. Employees are energized by working together in informal team settings that yield real results.

———

Whenever he meets staff, Horst Schulze, CEO of the Atlanta-based Ritz-Carlton Hotel Company, asks every employee in all de-

SUGGESTION BOX

☛ Conduct meetings around specific issues and brainstorm solutions.

☛ Determine what kind of meeting it is, and who should be there. Some meetings require all team members to be present. Others are better if only those individuals who are needed or who have something to contribute are invited.

☛ Assign roles and alternates for each meeting—for example, time keeper, recorder, and process monitor.

☛ Show respect for meeting participants—start and end meetings on time, even if some participants are late.

☛ Be ruthless about interruptions. Don't let team members cut each other off. Don't allow phone calls or other outside interruptions to disrupt your meetings.

☛ A team is only as good as its performance. Make sure there is a system for tracking action items and due dates.

> **"You can work or you can meet—you can't do both."**
>
> PETER DRUCKER
> Management Guru

partments two questions: "In six months, what do *you* want to become?" and "In six months, what do you want your *department* to become?" From employees all around the world, Schulze gets the same answer to both questions: "To become the *best!*" It's small wonder that Ritz-Carlton was the first service company to win the Malcolm Baldrige award for quality.

———

To ensure that everyone is in sync, employees at Maniker-Leiter & Associates, a management and organizational development consulting firm in Los Angeles, participate in a 10-minute "stand up" meeting at the beginning of each week to discuss each individual's focus for the week. Associates are energized by the opportunity to talk about their projects and the progress they have made.

———

Doctors and staff members at Linda Miles and Associates, a dental consulting firm in Virginia Beach, Virginia, donate half a day's earnings each month to a trip "kitty" that pays for their travel to major off-site meetings and office retreats. Staff members are energized by the retreats, which provide a break from the normal office routine in locations where they are uninterrupted by phone calls, clients, and visitors.

———

AirNet (formerly Timexpress), an air freight shipper in Columbus, Ohio, holds team meetings once every six weeks. Prior to the meetings, team members are asked to forward operations problems to the meeting's chairperson, who presents them to the group for resolution. Says operations manager Bruce Beacom, "This forum makes team members the beneficiaries of their own resolutions. The remarkable result is a cooperative spirit between operations and customer service.

———

Owens-Corning Fiberglass in Toledo, Ohio, uses "open-space" meetings to improve communication and productivity among team members. Pioneered by Episcopal priest and management consultant Harrison Owen, open-space meetings have no agenda, no planned sessions, and no scheduled speakers. The unstructured nature of this format energizes employees. Participants sit in a circle and anyone who is willing to lead a break-out session steps into the center of the circle and announces his or her name and topic. The topics are posted on the wall. Then everyone participates in as many break-out groups as they wish.

———

At the Knight-Ridder newspaper chain, based in Miami, management employs a variety of methods to ensure that information is distributed to everyone in the organization quickly and accurately. One of these methods is the "management coffee break," in which small teams of workers meet with top managers to get briefed on the latest organizational news and to ask questions.

———

Rules of the Game

Jack Stack, the President and CEO of engine rebuilder SRC Corporation, developed an employee-empowerment program known as the "Great Game of Business." Four of its tenets are:

1. We want to live up to our end of the employment bargain.

2. We want employees to seek new challenges by thinking about where they want to go in their work and their lives, instead of getting trapped in the same old routines.

3. We want to get rid of the "employee" mentality. Each person thinks and acts like an owner.

4. We want to create and distribute wealth. Productivity improves as employees work to create an organization based on continuous improvement and on helping one another.

> **❝Delegating means letting others become the experts and hence the best.❞**
>
> TIMOTHY W. FIRNSTAHL
> CEO, Restaurant Services, Inc.

A rmed with a huge stack of company reports, the financial department of Ameritech, a telecommunications company in Chicago, hit the road to visit every major branch office. In face-to-face meetings, the headquarters team held up each report and ask the field managers, "Do you really need this?" While some reports were deemed useful, a number of them were consolidated and others were dropped altogether—resulting in the elimination of the production and circulation of more than six million pages of reports, as well as in time freed-up for other tasks among the employees who were previously burdened with reading them all.

———

A t General Electric's Bayamón, Puerto Rico, lightning arrester plant, employees are organized into teams that are responsible for specific plant functions—shipping, assembly, and so forth. Teams consist of employees from all parts of the plant, enabling representatives from all affected departments to discuss how suggested changes or improvements will affect their part of the operation. Hourly workers—or *associates*—run meetings on their own, and *advisers*—formerly called managers—intervene only at the request of the team. The approach is successful. A year after startup, the plant's employees measured a full 20 percent higher in productivity than their closest counterpart in the mainland United States.

———

Team Initiative

Just as new challenges can energize an individual employee, teams of employees can be energized when they take the responsibility to initiate a new task or solve a long-standing problem. As the members of a team work together, they develop relationships with one another and build an energized and cohesive unit that can pull together to meet almost any challenge. For the members of the team, going above and beyond the call of duty becomes routine, instead of an isolated event.

At the Tennant Company, a manufacturer of flow maintenance products and equipment in Minneapolis, Minnesota, engineers devised a $100,000 system to streamline a particular welding operation. When management decided that the system was too expensive, a small group of welders tackled the problem and devised an overhead monorail system out of I-beams from a local junkyard for less than $2,000. The system saved more than $29,000 in production time and storage space, and the team of welders was energized by the initiative they had taken to solve the problem.

> **❝**The work of a business, of a government bureaucracy, of most forms of human activity, is something pursued not by individuals but by teams.**❞**
>
> ANDREW GROVE
> President and CEO, Intel

Team initiative can sometimes do more than simply energize the members of the team—it can save jobs. When the main operating face at an Amax coal mine was close to running out of material, management of the Gillette, Wyoming-based company decided that the

❝All good work is done in defiance of management.❞

BOB WOODWARD
Reporter

$24 million consultants estimated was needed to keep the operation in production was uneconomical. A company engineer casually met with the miners and put together a team of volunteers to consider other options. Meeting on Saturdays, the team developed a plan that cost only $4.8 million. It worked like a charm.

The design team for a locomotive at Fairfield, Connecticut-based General Electric was explicitly told four times by management to "cease and desist" in their efforts. However, because of their energy and commitment, the members of the team continued their work anyway and succeeded in developing a locomotive that now accounts for a significant portion of the company's total business.

The IBM personal computer was developed by a team of 12 employees given the task of getting IBM into the personal computer business as soon as possible. The team was given the authority to override standard company procedures as necessary to get the job done. This unique and energizing arrangement, which emphasized the team members' initiative, resulted in the first commercially successful personal computer—the model for most personal computers produced to this day.

Employees who are allowed to control their own work are energized employees. At electronics manufacturer Motorola, in Schaumberg, Illinois, *all* employees are expected to play key roles in the management of the firm. Says vice president Rick Chandler, "My workers are my managers whether they're in purchasing or production. So I have 1,000 managers. I have more managers than anybody else I ever met in my life. They determine when and how they should have a team, who goes in and who goes out."

Employee volunteers at Com-Corp Industries, a metal stamping company in Cleveland, Ohio, formed a committee to survey the marketplace to determine what other manufacturers were paying their employees. The employees were energized when they were allowed to set their own wages, according to their findings.

Employees at Nashville-based Management 21, a management consulting firm, completed an eight-hour outdoor adventure filled with team-building activities. The highlight of the day was completing a 40-foot ropes course with a partner. According to client liaison Cheryle Jaggers, "The team becomes energized and a can-do attitude becomes the norm."

By putting together a small team of workers, and encouraging them to take the initiative to solve problems, helicopter parts manufacturer Lord Aerospace Products Division of the Lord Corporation in Dayton, Ohio, energized the rest of the company's employees. Productivity went up 30 percent and absenteeism dropped 75 percent.

SUGGESTION BOX

☛ *Provide employee teams ample opportunity to work together to solve problems.*

☛ *Encourage and defend minority opinions, even if it means explaining and developing two different parallel ideas at once.*

☛ *Quickly accept and implement team recommendations whenever feasible.*

CASE STUDY:
TRUSTING EMPLOYEES AT RHINO FOODS

At Burlington, Vermont-based Rhino Foods, energizing employees starts at the top—specifically, with founder and president Ted Castle. One way that he shows his commitment to them is through a heavy emphasis on teams and teamwork.

At Rhino, the company that supplies chocolate-chip cookie dough to Ben & Jerry's for its ice cream, teams are involved in almost every aspect of the business. When a new team is about to be formed, or when an established team needs a new member, the company posts an "opportunity" bulletin. This bulletin—which describes the exact details of the team posting and the required level of commitment—notifies all employees that a project opening exists.

Volunteers are never hard to find. When director of human resources, Marlene Dailey, decided to form a team of production workers to hire new employees, she posted an opportunity bulletin. Despite the fact that a minimum one-year commitment was required and that the time spent on the team would be in addition to the employees' existing responsibil-

ities, she quickly had four volunteers. After sitting in on numerous real interviews, and receiving training in interviewing techniques, etiquette, and the legal constraints of the hiring process, the team was ready to take on its task. Because team members had a vested interest in choosing the best workers, the company also benefited by getting the best new-hires possible.

Effective Meetings

Meetings are another way that employees at Rhino Foods stay involved and connected to the firm. No matter how busy its production schedule is, every other week Rhino shuts down operations for at least half an hour for a company meeting in which employees are informed about issues that affect them and are given a voice in making decisions.

For example, when the company decided to put together a 401(k) retirement plan, three 401(k) vendors were invited to make presentations to employees. After the meeting, the employees voted to determine which vendor the company would use. According to Dailey, "These kinds of meetings really make a difference—people get to know what's going on in the company and feel connected to it."

Innovative Solutions to Tough Problems

Even—perhaps, *especially*—when the going gets tough, management makes a point of involving its employees in solving its problems. Never was this clearer than when the company experienced a serious downturn in business, and 25 percent of its workforce was scheduled for layoff. A team of 26 employees volunteered to find a way to keep the affected employees on staff.

> Problems are seen as opportunities for breakthroughs, not occasions to blame.

Their solution was both innovative and effective. Instead of laying off employees, the company asked for volunteers to work as paid employees at local firms that needed temporary help. Rhino guaranteed the volunteers' jobs as long as they performed well in their temporary positions, and agreed to maintain their seniority and benefits. The new companies paid the volunteers' wages; Rhino made up the difference for those employees who had to take a pay cut at their new jobs.

Was the employee-designed program successful? You bet it was! Not only did the company avoid a nasty layoff, but the volunteers enjoyed the time in their new positions and gained perspective from the change of scene. Stephen Mayo, a quality assurance technician and one of the volunteers, says, "People ask me if I'd do it again. In a heartbeat. It's like a vacation: You go somewhere a few months knowing you're eventually coming home. And it's nice to get back home." Human resource director Dailey adds, "It was really effective during a potentially devastating time... it ended up cementing the team."

A Positive Outlook

One thing that can sap the energy of employees—no matter how committed they are—is working in an environment of blame. At Rhino, problems are seen as opportunities for breakthroughs—not occasions to blame employees for messing up their jobs. Castle says, "We look at problems as challenges to make things better." In this climate, instead of giving orders and exacting punishment, higher-ups focus on working with employees to develop solutions.

Team Suggestions

Although suggestions from individuals are very important to an organization, teams of employees can take on much larger problems than any one employee can. When Equitable Insurance's CEO Dick Jenrette needed to reduce annual operating costs by $100 million, he called key employees into a room and asked them how to do it. Within a couple of days, the employees made suggestions that resulted in a reduction of $162 million.

> **❝I** want people to get what's in their heads into our shareholders' pocketbooks and have a good time doing it.❞
>
> Lou Noto
> President and CEO,
> Mobil Oil Company

GE Mobile Communications introduced the concept of Win Teams to its plant in Lynchburg, Virginia. The teams, made up of volunteer employees, were encouraged to make any suggestions for improvements that stayed within company safety and quality standards, and then to budget for them as they saw fit—all without management approval. The 36 Win Teams generated 1,164 new suggestions in the first year, resulting in $7.1 million in savings to the company.

At Physio-Control, a cardiac-care equipment manufacturer in Redmond, Washington, employees work a four-day week as a result of a suggestion made by a group of production technicians.

An employee team at Penton Publishing in Cleveland, Ohio, suggested offering customers six or eight different types of paper instead of giving them an unlimited choice. As a result, the company has saved more than $1 million in paper costs.

———

At First Tennessee National, a bank holding company located in Memphis, a group of seven employees responsible for producing 1,400 monthly customer statements said they needed an occasional day off to take care of errands and other personal business. Knowing that they were more effective earlier in the month, the employees proposed a work schedule that exchanged a few 11-hour days in the beginning of each month for one day off later in the month. Management agreed and the plan was implemented. As a result, the time needed to issue the monthly statements was reduced from eight days to four, and both customer satisfaction and employee morale climbed.

———

At many firms, no-shows and employees on sick leave cost the company dearly. At United Airlines, headquartered in Chicago, a special team of employees chartered to consider the employee dependability problem recommended that the company be more flexible in allowing employees to swap assignments with one another. As a result, sick time was down 17 percent in 1995, resulting in a savings of $18.2 million. Workers' compensation claims have also fallen 17 percent and employee grievances have been dramatically reduced.

———

SUGGESTION BOX

☞ Encourage the formation of ad hoc teams of employees to address organizational problems.

☞ Make a point of personally speaking with every team that submits a suggestion to see what can be done to implement it.

☞ Create a climate of improvement by encouraging all employee suggestions, whether they have a big or small impact on the organization or its customers.

CASE STUDY:
BRAINSTORMING SUGGESTIONS AT FIRST MARYLAND BANCORP

The promise of improvements in morale and energy makes employee empowerment and suggestion programs attractive, but many companies wonder whether the benefits of such programs will outweigh the costs. This was certainly a question for the management of First Maryland Bancorp in Baltimore when it was considering adopting its "Brainstorm" program. To everyone's delight, Brainstorm cost less than $3 million to implement, and resulted in approximately $24 million in measurable savings to the firm.

Concentrated Suggestions

The problem with many suggestion programs is that employee enthusiasm drops quickly, and along with this drop in employee enthusiasm comes a reduction in the number and quality of suggestions. Instead of being an ongoing program like those found in many organizations, Brainstorm was specifically designed to last twelve weeks, and the committees formed to review employee suggestions were encouraged to decide on them within seven days of their submission. By limiting the program to 12 weeks, the bank was able to maintain enthusiasm throughout and to ensure the generation of high-quality suggestions.

Employees were encouraged to get together in teams to come up with ideas for increasing revenues or decreasing expenses. Team members investigated the potential improvements and developed quantitative justifications supporting their assessments. In other words, it wasn't enough for a team to say, "We suggest that Saturday work hours be cut back." To be accepted by the Brainstorm program, the suggestion had to be accompanied by a detailed cost/benefit analysis showing how much money was likely to be saved if the idea were implemented.

Management required employees to maintain all their duties throughout the process. In some companies, when suggestion programs are rolled out, performance suffers as employees begin to spend more time on committees than they do on their own jobs. At First Maryland, employees were encouraged to participate in the Brainstorm process during spare time at work or after normal working hours. Management made it clear that as important as the program was, taking care of the company's day-to-day business and customers was still the first priority.

Keys to Success

Four key factors led to Brainstorm's success:

- Top management agreed to support the program and the suggestions that came out of it. This is a key factor in any employee suggestion program: Once workers realize management is indifferent, the program will quickly lose credibility and employee support.

- The program had a big kick-off. CEO Charles W. Cole recorded a personal video message communicating his commitment for all employees and participated in numerous meetings to introduce the effort. He also made it clear that no employee would be penalized as a result of suggestions he or she made.

- Program coordinators, leaders of suggestion teams, and members of the suggestion evaluation committee were all given training before the program was rolled out. Any such program's credibility will be compromised if the initial efforts by those in charge are stumbling and tentative.

- Employees were given rewards for their suggestions. Of the $3 million or so spent on the program, about $2 million went to rewards.

Based on employee suggestions, First Maryland came up with more efficient ways to route telecommunications circuits; eliminate the distribution of large computer-generated reports to employees who no longer had any use for them; and reduce maintenance costs on computer equipment at branch banks.

With a payoff approximately eight times greater than the amount invested, the program was a tremendous success financially. However, according to senior vice president Brian King, the program would have been considered a success even if employees hadn't come up with any suggestions. Why? Because it taught employees the cost of doing business and they began to make better decisions about how to spend the company's resources. In addition, employees became more entrepreneurial, more creative, and more aware of the company's bottom line.

> **"Manufacturing excellence results from dedication to daily progress. Making something a little bit better every day."**
>
> ROBERT HALL
> Professor,
> Indiana University

At Mary Kay Cosmetics in Dallas, teams are now a way of life and employees are energized by having their ideas and suggestions heard and seriously considered. Creative Action Teams (CAT) were instrumental in launching Mary Kay Cosmetics in Japan, in planning the company's 30th anniversary celebration, and in developing a savings plan for sales directors. "They listen to you in the CATs," says Southwest distribution supervisor Tina Lynch. "Nothing gets thrown out. Everything is weighed. It may be a crazy idea or it may be a time-consuming idea, but they really do listen."

Work-Outs are General Electric's unique system of soliciting and implementing suggestions from employees (see page 27). Employees in a Work-Out team at GE's Louisville, Kentucky, appliance manufacturing plant found a unique way to illustrate the problem they were experiencing with high heat and humidity in the plant. The team led their boss, Jeff Svoboda, outside to the parking lot in 90-degree weather. As they took their time setting up an easel and flip charts, Svoboda was stuck standing in the sun. It didn't take him long to get the message and he quickly approved their proposal to open plant vents and to purchase and install additional ventilating fans and blowers.

Employees are often energized when suggestion programs include an incentive. During the month of December the suggestion program committee at Northern States Power in Eau Claire, Wisconsin, distributes wrapped Christmas gifts to everyone who has made suggestions during the previous year. Suggestions increased by 350 percent over the previous year, and this special promotion has become an employee favorite.

———

When an employee complained about the company's low wages to Rick Hartsock, the owner of Sandstrom Products, a manufacturer of specialty coatings in Port Byron, Illinois, Hartsock invited the disgruntled worker to form a pay-plan committee with his co-workers. Seven months later, the committee presented Hartsock with a new pay-for-knowledge plan that lets employees work their way from $10 to $15 an hour by learning new skills. The plan was quickly implemented.

———

Sometimes it takes a conducive space to generate great suggestions. At Kaiser Permanente Medical Care Program, a health-maintenance organization in Pasadena, California, a team of laboratory managers collaborated to convert a little-used conference room into a Strategy Center. The idea was to create an environment where freewheeling thinking could flourish and ideas would be generated. To accomplish this goal, the team purchased inexpensive but comfortable furniture and assembled it themselves, and equipped the room with a computer, printer, a white board that gener-

I-Power Ideas

Martin Edelston's book *I-Power* offers a system that facilitates the sugestion collecting process:

1. Prepare a short suggestion form and have it readily available at every meeting and at key locations throughout the organization.

2. Put a receptacle on the table into which people can drop ideas they have during meetings.

3. Once a week, retrieve the forms and affix them to sheets of three-hole-punched paper. Put all ideas submitted by an individual together. Place the pages in a three-ring binder.

4. Review all the ideas, comment, and ask for more information if necessary at least once a week—*without fail.*

5. As soon as an idea is accepted, personally reward the person who made the suggestion.

6. Prepare a monthly staff report on suggestions received and progress made in implementing accepted suggestions.

> **"**We don't feel that wages are the primary motivator. The real motivation is when the worker feels he's making a contribution.**"**
>
> RUSSELL CULOMB
> Plant Manager,
> General Electric

ates copies, and even a fake window. The room has been used extensively by teams of employees to address work-related issues, such as how to improve laboratory communications, and for brainstorming sessions. The Strategy Center is working so well that there are plans to create similar rooms in other Kaiser facilities.

———

Not long ago, it was not uncommon for United Airlines aircraft to burn jet fuel while idling at airport gates. While electricity was available at the gates as an option, ramp workers weren't using it—and they were wasting costly fuel in the process. A team of pilots, ramp workers, and managers worked together to attack the problem of fuel conservation and arrived at an elegantly simple, but effective solution to the problem. Ramp workers complained that they weren't able to plug the electrical cables into the aircraft because the ladders on the ramp were usually too short to reach. By purchasing longer ladders and placing them at all United gates, the company was able to save $20 million in fuel costs in one year alone.

———

Creative Teams

All employees can use a boost to their creativity from time to time, and the same goes for teams. This requires a bit more planning and logistical foresight than when working with only one or two employees at a time, but it can be well worth the effort. Simply taking the team out of the work environment or asking members to look at a problem from a different vantage can do the trick. And sometimes just letting a team of employees tackle a tough issue on its own—without the intervention of management—can often energize the group and boost creativity at the same time.

When his team needs a dose of energy, J. Allard, a unit manager at software giant Microsoft, takes them to the company basketball court to shoot some hoops and toss around ideas.

Sometimes, simply taking employees out of their daily routines can dramatically increase their energy and creativity. One morning, Mike Vargas, a Hewlett-Packard employee, awoke to find a subpoena under his door, summoning him for jury duty. It was the first step in an elaborate "trial" conducted by the electronics company's integrated circuit division to determine the fate of its new business plan. On one side, a team of employees argued the case against the plan. On the other side, another team of employees defended the plan. A 90-member jury made up of a

> 66All the companies that are alive are realizing that they need more creative, vital, and adaptable workers.99
>
> DAVID WHYTE
> *The Heart Aroused:*
> *Poetry and Preservation of the*
> *Soul of Corporate America*

SUGGESTION BOX

☛ *Give employees the time and the place to be creative.*

☛ *Spend some team meetings brainstorming solutions to only one key organizational problem.*

☛ *Have one member of the team come up with an idea, and then pass it on to the next team member to add his or her ideas. Continue in this fashion until all team members have made a contribution.*

variety of employees completed the courtroom "cast." After each side had presented its arguments during the course of the two-day trial, the jury found in favor of the new plan.

———

Kathe Farris, reward-and-recognition consultant for the Bank of Boston, grants each member of her staff four "informational days" per year. The days are set aside to work on special projects of the employee's choosing, and they are allowed to work on their projects either in the office or offsite. Says Farris, "Due to our fast-paced environment, we often never get to 'special' projects or topics of interest. The informational days provide at least four opportunities per year to do that!"

———

Working outside of official channels, a group of software engineers at Xerox Corporation, headquartered in Stamford, Connecticut, banded together to form the Toolkit Working Group. In three years, the group created a new innovation—reusable software code—that the official company task forces had still not accomplished after five years of trying.

———

To challenge thinking, and to spur the energy and creativity of its employees, Honda Motors in Tokyo deliberately places individuals who know nothing about technology on the company's design teams. Great innovations arise from the spirited discussions that flow from the "I know nothing" questions and probing.

———

CASE STUDY:
PATHS TO EMPOWERMENT AT 3M

At 3M (Minnesota Mining & Manufacturing), a diversified manufacturer with more than $13 billion in annual sales, creativity is just about the most important attribute an employee can have. To spur innovation, for example, the St. Paul-based company encourages members of its technical and engineering staffs to spend some of their work time pursuing projects of their own choosing.

Maximizing Employee Creativity

But as CEO Livio DeSimone recognizes, you can't force your employees to be creative. Creativity thrives when employees are given the freedom and the time to be creative. As DeSimone puts it, "A business trying to do new things doesn't lend itself well to regimentation." Here is DeSimone's ten-point plan for maximizing creativity and productivity.

1. Give folks time and space to follow their muse. 3M not only allows but encourages its technical employees to devote 15 percent of their work time to their own research projects. Some employees spend up to 50 percent of their time on their own projects. Not only does this practice energize and empower employees, it leads to "happy accidents" such as Post-it® Notes—a product line that brings more than $100 million into the company every year.

2. Create a culture of cooperation. At 3M, employees are encouraged to ignore departmental boundaries and collaborate with one another—whether in person, or via phone, or e-mail.

3. Measure your results. Among the things 3M measures are sales, earnings, market share, and new products. As a basic goal, DeSimone asks that new products account for 30 percent of business unit sales.

4. Stay ahead of the customer. Good communication between 3M employees and customers is required in order to define what customers need—often even before they know they need it.

Continued on next page.

5. Stage celebrations. Employee recognition is an important part of 3M's strategy for energizing employees. The pinnacle of employee awards is induction into the Carlton Society, the company's hall of fame.

6. Be honest and know when to say no. At 3M, managers are open to new ideas from employees throughout the organization. However, some ideas don't make sense for one reason or another. In these cases, managers are encouraged to be direct and up-front in telling their employees.

7. Make the company a lifetime career. Layoffs at 3M are rare, and most 3M managers have been with the company for 25 years or longer.

8. Give your best managers overseas assignments. While at some companies such an assignment can mean putting one's career into the doldrums, DeSimone is a big believer in using foreign postings to round out the experience of his executives. In fact, 75 percent of 3M's top 135 executives have lived overseas for three years or more.

9. Keep increasing research and development spending. For the last 20 years straight, 3M has continued to up the ante on its R&D spending. With more than 6.5 percent of its revenues, or approximately $875 million, devoted to research and development, 3M is sure to continue to spur its employees to new heights of creativity and innovation.

10. Don't believe everything Wall Street tells you. "I can remember back in the '80s when every security analyst said, 'You ought to leverage your company a lot more. You should borrow a lot more money,' " says DeSimone. "But we're sitting back here in the Midwest—you know, farmer types. And our answer is, 'We don't think that's a safe thing to do.' And now we look back on it, and we see that a lot of the companies that leveraged the hell out of themselves are either not around anymore or have gone through horrendous times."

Teams Make It Happen

Of course, it's one thing to set goals for employee empowerment, and it's another thing to really make it happen. One of the ways that management at 3M makes sure that employees are empowered and energized is through the company's "action teams." Action teams are interdisciplinary groups of eight to ten people. When necessary advisors are called in to assist on specific topics or issues. The team leader is not a boss, but a facilitator, an equal member of the team who helps to identify critical issues and resolve conflict.

3M vice president Robert Hershock and corporate scientist David Braun formed an action team to figure out a way to dramatically compress development time for a new product. As a result of their experience they determined that a successful action team must possess the following three characteristics:

1. It must have a specific charter.

2. It must be highly focused.

3. It must be short-term and high-energy.

Here are some additional tips that Braun and Hershock learned from their experience with action teams:

■ Secure support and buy-in from senior management. At 3M, each action team is assigned a sponsor from the ranks of the company's senior management. It's the job of the team's sponsor to serve as a bridge between the team and management and to help remove roadblocks that may impede the team's progress.

> **"A business trying to do new things doesn't lend itself well to regimentation."**
>
> LIVIO DESIMONE, CEO

■ Carefully manage group size and composition. Membership on action teams shouldn't be left to chance. At 3M, prospective members are interviewed and only those candidates who show flexibility and the ability to cooperate are brought on board.

■ Commit to up-front planning. Plan the process. Lay out broad guidelines and parameters, then let the team innovate within those parameters.

■ Invest in team training. Team members often have to learn new skills to function successfully in a team environment. At 3M, members of action teams participate in a special three-day training session to work on interpersonal skills, conflict resolution techniques, and how to conduct meetings.

■ Make sure the team is working together well. Positive signs to look for are: full participation; strong leadership; decisions by consensus; a clear mission; enjoyment of the teamwork. Signs that all is not well include: silent or distracted members; hostility; wheel-spinning; majority rule; a single dominant leader or member; problem avoidance.

Self-Managed Work Teams

Imagine a workplace where all employees manage themselves. A place where everyone does their jobs without the need for supervision—where workers take responsibility for carrying out their duties efficiently and on time, set their own schedules, hire and fire co-workers, and determine their own pay. A place where employees are energized by the freedom of working as though the business belonged to them. Does this workplace sound like an impossible dream? It shouldn't. Self-managed teams at Published Image, a printing firm in Boston, halted chronically high employee turnover and increased the company's profit margin from 3 percent to 20 percent by setting their own work schedules, preparing their own budgets, and setting up their own reward systems. Across the country, self-managing work teams are doing all this and more. Right now.

> 66The modest-sized, task-oriented, semi-autonomous, mainly self-managing team should be the basic organizational building block.99
>
> TOM PETERS
> *Thriving on Chaos*

Belonging to a team that accomplishes what is seemingly impossible can be a very energizing experience. A multifunctional team made up of employees from accounting, manufacturing, marketing, and sales at the power-tool division of Ingersoll-Rand, headquartered in Woodcliff Lake, New Jersey, designed and produced an innovative hand-held grinder in only one year instead of the usual four.

Managers can energize team members—and teach them important self-management skills—when they avoid the temptation to solve their problems for them. When a work team at XEL, a telecommunications equipment manufacturer located near Denver, approached manager John Puckett to intervene in an employee dispute, it took a conscious effort on his part to resist doing what he had always done. Says Puckett, "I almost got sucked into solving their problem. Then I realized this wasn't my problem. So I went back to them and said, 'Look, this is part of the team's responsibility. You don't have the option of not working it out.'"

———

At First Union Brokerage Services of Charlotte, North Carolina, employees participate in their own recognition committee. The committee, which has no management involvement, has its own budget. Employees organize ways to recognize each other's accomplishments throughout the year, and each year, new committee members—energized by the experience of managing their own program—are responsible for submitting a business plan for the following year's programs.

———

The San Diego Zoo empowered its employees when it created teams to develop and run its special exhibits, such as the $7.5 million, 3½ acre Tiger River exhibit and the Sun Bear exhibit. Employees assigned to such teams have 30 percent fewer workers' compensation claims

Lattice, Not Ladders

W. L. Gore and Associates has dispensed with the traditional corporate hierarchy, instead organizing according to a "lattice" structure. (See page 120.) The key characteristics of such a structure are:

1. Lines of communication are direct—person to person—with no intermediaries.

2. There is no fixed or assigned authority.

3. There are sponsors, not bosses.

4. Natural leadership is defined by the "followership."

5. Objectives are set by those who must make them happen.

6. Employee commitments to one another and their projects drive their tasks and assignments.

Extend Your Neck

Tom McConnell, president of New England Securities Corporation, published the following guiding principles to liberate his employees from the fear of trying new things:

1. Take risks. Don't play it safe.

2. Make mistakes. Don't try to avoid them.

3. Take initiative. Don't wait for instructions.

4. Spend energy on solutions, not emotions.

5. Shoot for total quality. Don't shave standards.

6. Welcome destruction. It's the first step in the creative process.

7. Focus on opportunities, not problems.

8. Experiment.

9. Take personal responsibility for fixing things. Don't blame others.

10. Try easier, not harder.

11. Stay calm!

12. Smile.

13. Have fun!

and significantly lower absenteeism than non-team members. Says Sun Bear team leader John Michel, "The greatest benefit of the teams is the renewed enthusiasm and sense of responsibility and ownership felt by everyone. I have trouble getting people to leave work on time."

———

Self-directed work teams at Rheaco, an aerospace parts manufacturer in Grand Prairie, Texas, reduced the time needed to manufacture a brake shoe for the Lockheed C-130 military transport aircraft—a part that Rheaco had been manufacturing for 25 years—from 3½ hours to less than an hour by working together to plan and implement new efficiencies in the manufacturing process.

———

Workers can become energized when they are trusted with the responsibility for carrying out tasks that are normally within the province of management. The implementation of self-directed work teams at Aero Component Technologies in Ft. Walton Beach, Florida, has freed workers to make decisions that formerly belonged to management. The result is lower costs and better products. Says machine operator Joe Davis, "Before you had to go to somebody and ask what you had to do all the time. Now we do it ourselves, and we put out a better product."

———

Breaking the traditional mold of departments that specialize in certain tasks, the production side of flexible hose and fittings maker Titeflex in Springfield, Massachusetts, reorganized itself into 10- to 12-person autonomous Business Development Teams (BDTs). Teams buy and sell from one another and can take orders all the way from design to delivery.

A t Saturn, the innovative automotive division of General Motors located in Spring Hill, Tennessee, each employee team is assigned the duty of manufacturing a major system of the automobile. The teams function as independent small business units, with responsibility for their own accounting, budget, hiring, and relations with other teams. New employees receive 92 hours of training in empowerment and teamwork-related skills such as listening, creative thinking, management by consensus, and conflict resolution. Veteran employees set aside 5 percent of their total annual work hours for retraining.

A t Semco, a manufacturer of specialized electronic components in Willimantic, Connecticut, not only do factory workers get to set their own quotas and schedules, they help design the products they produce and develop their own marketing plans. When the company decided to relocate a factory, the company closed for the day to take all its workers on a tour of three possible sites and let them vote on which site to develop.

> **"Participative management is, simply stated, involving the right people at the right time in the decision process."**
>
> WAYNE BARLO
> Regional Administrator,
> FAA

A-Teams

According to a study by management expert Bob Culver, empowered teams are teams that:

1. Make the most of decisions that influence team success.

2. Choose their own leaders.

3. Add or remove team members when necessary.

4. Set their own goals and commitments.

5. Define and perform much of their own training.

6. Are rewarded as a team.

At Penn Parking, a parking garage management firm in Baltimore, Maryland, employees are allowed to decide for themselves who works when. Management assigns two people for every shift (when only one is needed). It is entirely up to the pair to decide who takes which days. Absenteeism and turnover are down and team spirit is up because employees determine their own schedules and are willing to cover for their partners when they know that the favor will be returned.

In many ways, self-managing work teams function as energized microbusinesses. At the spice giant McCormick & Company in Hunt Valley, Maryland, employee teams draw up their own budgets and make other decisions that directly affect their jobs. Team leader Gregg Black says, "All the responsibilities for the business are brought down to my level and even to the people who work for me. It's like we're entrepreneurs running our own business. It's our own cookie shop and we can control the waste, or how much time we spend working on a certain project."

Allowing teams to make their own decisions is energizing to all the members of the team. Aerospace giant Boeing, based in Seattle, has a "no messenger" rule. Team members must make decisions on the spot; they cannot run around looking for supervisors to make them. As a result of this policy, Boeing was able to build

its new 777-passenger jet with less than half the design glitches of any earlier jet program.

———

In 1966, General Foods turned its Gaines dog food plant in Topeka, Kansas, over to teams of workers, who were put in charge of company performance. Supervisory positions were abolished and teams set their own work hours, made their own assignments, and hired new team members. Workers were energized as they rotated through a variety of assignments throughout the plant and as financial information was shared freely. As absentee rates plunged to 2 percent, the Topeka plant set new performance records for General Foods.

———

At Waxahachie, Texas-based Baylor Medical Center, self-managing teams of nurses are empowered to determine their own schedules and do their own interviewing the hiring.

———

When hierarchies are broken down, employees often become more productive. At design firm IDEO Product Development in Palo Alto, California, there are no bosses or job titles. All work is done by teams that form and disband—after weeks or months—when projects begin and end. As a result of the freedom employees enjoy and their creativity, IDEO has become one of the most respected firms in the industry.

———

SUGGESTION BOX

☛ *Let teams decide their own purpose and ground rules.*

☛ *Rotate team leadership responsibilities among all team members.*

☛ *Set up a system for accountability and follow through.*

CARE

CASE STUDY:
THE LATTICE STRUCTURE AT
W.L. GORE AND ASSOCIATES

For some companies, energizing and empowering employees is not a new idea. From its founding more than 30 years ago, W.L. Gore and Associates, maker of the water-resistant Gore-Tex® fabric, electronic connectors, and other high-tech fabrics and products, has been a firm believer in trapping the energy, creativity, and organizational ability of its employees. The firm—with annual worldwide sales in the vicinity of nearly $1 billion—has held true to founder Bill Gore's belief in employee self-management and self-development, and the freedom of employees to communicate with anyone else in the organization.

Job Titles:
Who Needs Them?

At Gore, based in Newark, Delaware, all employees—known as associates—are part of one big team, or "lattice." There is no traditional hierarchy; rather, the company is organized as a loose network of employees who are all responsible to each other and to their projects.

Bill Gore dubbed this democratic style of management "lattice" because of what he observed at traditional companies. "Every underground organization has an underground lattice," he said. "It's where news spreads like lightning, where people can go around the organization to get things done." A lattice organization is based on employees being interconnected and all at the same level. Decisions are made throughout the organization instead of from the top down.

Because there is no hierarchy, associates manage themselves, and leaders usually emerge from the ranks of associates rather than being appointed. Instead of having workers and bosses, there are associates and sponsors. Sponsors champion associates in one of three ways:

Starting sponsors help new associates get started in their jobs. They also assist employees who change jobs within the company.

Advocate sponsors make sure that the associates in their charge get credit for their accomplishments and contributions to the company.

Compensation sponsors ensure

that associates' pay is commensurate with their contributions.

All associates have at least one sponsor and many of them have more than one.

In addition to all employees being part of one big team, smaller, cross-functional teams are always being formed to carry out specific tasks and projects. For associates up to the challenge of an ever-changing organization, the lattice framework is very liberating and energizing.

A New Kind of Leadership

Despite the lack of formal managers at Gore, leadership is absolutely critical to the success of the organization. In an internal memo, Bill Gore described the kind of leader needed at the company:

1. The associate who is recognized by a team as having special knowledge or experience. (A chemist, computer expert, machine operator, salesman, engineer, or lawyer.) This kind of leader gives the team guidance in a special area.

2. The associate the team looks to for coordination of individual activities in order to achieve the agreed-upon objectives of the team. The role of this leader is to persuade team members to make the commitments necessary for success.

3. The associate who proposes objectives and activities and seeks team consensus. This leader is perceived by the team members as having a good grasp of how the objectives of the team fit in with the broad objective of the enterprise. (This kind of leader is often also a "commitment seeking" leader as in No. 2 above.)

The lattice structure allows those associates with leadership ability to naturally take on more responsibility in areas that they're good at.

When, for whatever reason, a leader doesn't work out, he or she can be easily reabsorbed into the team. For example, when a company technical expert was hired into a team as a production leader, it took six months for him to realize that he preferred his old role over his new one. By returning to his old job, the expert gained an extra measure of respect from his peers.

> In a lattice structure, there is no hierarchy. Employees are responsible to each other and their projects.

Sam's Rules

Sam Walton, the founder of retailing giant Wal-Mart, wrote 10 rules for building a business—most of them centered around ways to energize employees. Here they are:

1. Commit to your business.

2. Share your profits with all associates, and treat them as partners.

3. Motivate your partners.

4. Communicate everything you possibly can to your partners.

5. Appreciate everything your associates do for the business.

6. Celebrate your successes.

7. Listen to everyone in your company.

8. Exceed your customers' expectations.

9. Control your expenses better than your competition does.

10. Swim upstream.

The process of transforming a workforce from an old-fashioned, hierarchical structure to a more democratic employee-managed one can be very energizing to employees. To improve customer service and reduce costs, Minneapolis's *Star Tribune* newspaper company decided to switch from managing its workforce with the traditional, high-control style, to implementing self-managed teams. The result was the reduction of department supervisors—from 23 to 8—and the delegation of tasks formerly reserved for management to lower-level employees. Billing mistakes were cut in half, and the number of customers lost due to poor service was reduced from 362 one year to 52 the next.

At Whole Foods Market, a chain of health food stores based in Austin, Texas, all employees at the company's 43 stores are energized by belonging to one or more teams. Each department—produce, grocery, baking—is run by its own self-managed team of employees. The team leaders from each store constitute a team, as do the store leaders from each region, and the six regional vice presidents. In its 16 years of existence, Whole Foods has become the largest natural-foods grocer in the United States.

In many organizations, secretaries have little autonomy and the opportunities for them to become energized are few and far between. At Corning, a glass- and kitchenware company in

Corning, New York, a group of secretaries got together and announced to management that they wanted to set up their new office space. The secretaries were allowed to choose the colors of the walls, design and set up the kitchens and service centers, and organize the move itself. Secretary Kathy Foley, an employee since 1966, says, "Here you can voice your opinion and you are heard."

———

PART III

ENERGIZING ORGANIZATIONS

Every company begins with energy. A simple idea, a successful product or service, a small group of determined individuals committed to turning a vision into a reality. In the beginning, everybody has multiple jobs and every employee is expected to take the initiative to do what is right without being told. But somewhere along the way, as an organization grows and prospers, the excitement diffuses. Management becomes distant from the customer, more focused on making the quarterly numbers, improving inventory turnover, and analyzing financial rates than on inspiring employees to do their best. Employees often become more complacent as their jobs become more predictable. The thrill of new opportunities is replaced with controlled growth, professional management, and strict policies and procedures that can reduce employee initiative to finding the right page in the policy manual.

The nature of an organization plays a tremendous role in energizing or de-energizing employees. The organization can be flexible—systematically providing options, resources, and tools to help managers energize their employees—or it can be bureaucratic and policy-bound, creating an atmosphere that erodes the confidence, self-esteem, and energy of its employees.

Fortunately, management can reawaken and revive the spirit that initially made the company great by paying attention to the aspects of the organization that stifle individual initiative and creativity and changing or eliminating those practices. An organization's policies and procedures, working environment, facilities, and the opportunities and challenges made available to employees all help to determine how they feel about their employers, and whether or not they will give their best effort to their jobs. This section presents examples of how innovative companies are energizing individuals and encouraging individual initiative through their organizational practices.

Policies and Procedures

Many companies today are discovering an easy way to energize their employees: They simply throw out the volumes of policies and procedures that hamstring the efforts of energized employees and replace them with simpler, less restrictive versions. Smart organizations realize that employees can be trusted to do what's right when they are allowed to take responsibility for their actions. When Dayton Power & Light in Dayton, Ohio, renegotiated their contract with their employees' union, it was shortened from 200 pages to 14—the first page being a statement of shared philosophy. Since the change, management and workers are energized to work together to confront problems. Similarly, after Johnsonville Foods in Sheboygan Falls, Wisconsin, created a new organizational structure—with little hierarchy, substantial employee involvement, and a profit-sharing program, the company's market share in the Milwaukee area rocketed from 7 percent to 50 percent within 10 years.

A few years ago, Houston-based Continental Airlines symbolically burned its legalistic, several-hundred-page policies and procedures manual and replaced it with a relatively short document titled "Working Together Guidelines." The new guidelines rely on "the judgment of the people who really run this airline," that is, line employees.

> **❝Programs don't make quality products, people do.❞**
>
> JOHN PETERMAN
> Owner, The J. Peterman
> Company

SUGGESTION BOX

☞ *When it comes to policies, shorter and simpler is better than bigger and more complex.*

☞ *Every time you establish a new policy, get rid of two old policies.*

☞ *Make sure that your organization's policies and procedures are written to serve your employees and customers—not just the organization.*

☞ *Beware of establishing a new policy or procedure in reaction to a single incident—the problem may never arise again.*

☞ *No matter the size of the organization, no single policy should take up more than a page.*

A key belief of the Toledo, Ohio-based auto parts manufacturer Dana Corporation is stated in its one-page corporate policy statement: "The people who know best how the job should be done are the ones doing it."

———

From its founding, electronics manufacturer Hewlett-Packard, in Palo Alto, California, has encouraged innovation, risk taking, and the freedom to fail honorably. Included in its principles of operation, called "The H-P Way," is this statement: "We reserve the right to make mistakes." In addition, besides offering employees one of the best pay and benefits packages in American industry, Hewlett-Packard implemented the Friday night beer bust, invented flextime, eradicated time clocks, and developed the concept of "management by wandering around."

———

On the first page of Viking Freight System's employee handbook, the San Jose, California-based company sets the tone: "Most people spend approximately one-third of their adult life working. Viking was founded on the idea that anything to which a person dedicates that much of his or her life should be enjoyed."

———

Every page of the handbook that Bentonville, Arkansas-based retail giant Wal-Mart gives to its associates—Wal-Mart's term for "employee"—has the header "We're glad you're here," and the footer "Our PEOPLE make the difference." And if the associates aren't satisfied with the way the chain of command within their store deals with a problem, they are encouraged to call corporate headquarters.

———

When a company's policies show compassion, it can be energizing to employees. At Gene's Books in King-of-Prussia, Pennsylvania, employees can give each other unused sick days when catastrophic illnesses or other personal emergencies occur.

———

In a visit to a utility company to study its best practices, teams from Sprint Corporation in Westwood, Kansas, were shocked to learn that some corporate cultures weren't quite as rigid as theirs. When the Sprint teams asked questions regarding dress code and attendance policies, the firm responded that its policies were "come to work," and "wear clothes." According to Sprint benchmarking manager Jeff Amen, "We got the biggest whack on the side of the head by the answers to those two questions. We were surprised to discover their attendance policy was not 28 pages long like ours! We obviously had a long way to go to say it in three words!"

———

Specialty-dessert maker Rhino Foods "walks its talk" when it comes to employee participation in decision making. Here is the Burlington,

Welcome to Nordstrom

Seattle, Washington-based clothing retailer Nordstrom has a distinct aversion to voluminous employee policies. Here, almost in its entirety, is Nordstrom's employee handbook:

We're glad to have you with our Company.

Our number-one goal is to provide outstanding customer service.

Set both your personal and professional goals high.

We have great confidence in your ability to achieve them.

❝Most people *want* to do well. When people don't feel good and don't do well in an organization, the problem is usually the way the organization is structured.❞

DR. MITCHELL RABKIN
President, Beth Israel
Hospital, Boston

Vermont-based company's Employee Principle section of its purpose statement:

> **"The employees and families of Rhino Foods are its greatest assets. The company's relationship with its employees is founded on a climate of mutual trust and respect, within an environment for listening and personal expression. Rhino Foods declares that it is a vehicle for its people to get what they want."**

To help break down barriers between employees, First Federal Bank of California, based in Santa Monica, has a written policy requiring employees to operate on a first-name basis.

Employees at Delta Land Surveying and Engineering, in Flint, Michigan, vote at least once a year on matters such as dress codes, bonuses, and moonlighting rules.

AT&T, headquartered in New York City, eliminated most of its company travel policies in favor of an elegantly simple new corporate travel statement: "Use your good judgment, always keeping the shareholder in mind."

The personnel policy statement for Polaroid, a photographic and digital imaging systems products manufacturer in Cambridge, Massachusetts, defines two inseparable, basic company products: (1) "Products that are genuinely unique and useful," and (2) "A worthwhile working life for each member of the Company."

Sunnyvale, California-based computer consulting firm Scitor Corporation demonstrates its trust in its employees by refusing to set a maximum number of days for employee sick leave. Scitor workers average five days of sick leave a year, less than the industry average.

Tandem Computers in Cupertino, California, has a dual-track reward system that allows employees to gain promotions based on technical *or* managerial merit. It also has a philosophy department that helps to ensure that all 10,000 employees understand the company's values and vision.

At Pitney Bowes, the Stamford, Connecticut-based office equipment manufacturer, employees who feel they have been treated unfairly have access to a corporate ombudsman. The ombudsman's services are completely confidential.

Pride Principles

Insurance leader USAA of San Antonio, Texas, embraces 10 PRIDE principles to help the company—*and* employees—achieve its goals. They are:

- **Exceed customer expectations.** Every contact is an opportunity to demonstrate our commitment to service.
- **Live the Golden Rule.** Treat others with courtesy and respect.
- **Be a leader.** Everyone can be one, even if you lead only yourself.
- **Participate and contribute.** The success of USAA is everyone's responsibility.
- **Pursue excellence.**
- **Work as a team.** Teamwork promotes innovation and creativity.
- **Share knowledge.**
- **Keep it simple.** Make it easy for our customers to do business with us and for us to work together.
- **Listen and communicate.** Our customers and our co-workers deserve our best.
- **Have fun.** If you're not, figure out why not and change it.

Fostering Independence and Autonomy

While employees are often willing to take on many of the duties normally left to management—budgeting, hiring, firing, and so forth—they need a clear signal from their employers in order to make the transition to self-management. Once they do start managing themselves, the positive effect on the organization can be astounding. For example, when management at the Polo Ralph Lauren distribution center in Greensboro, North Carolina, decided to let employees determine for themselves when to take their breaks and lunch hours, productivity shot up 20 percent. Time and again organizations that encourage employee independence and autonomy find that they energize their employees while improving the bottom line.

> **❝**Real motivation comes from within. People have to be given the freedom to succeed or fail.**❞**
>
> GORDON FORWARD
> CEO, Chaparral Steel

The inside cover of a recent annual report for Bloomington, Minnesota-based Apogee Enterprises, a holding company that includes Harmon Glass and Wausau Metals, highlighted this quote: "We don't believe in bureaucracy. Apogee's hallmark is decentralized management, and decisions are made as close to the customer as possible."

Despite the fact that Chaparral Steel's products are top quality, the Midlothian, Texas, company refuses to use quality inspectors. Says CEO Gordon Forward, "The people in our plants are responsible for their own product and its quality. We expect them to act like owners."

———

Employees at Meredith Publishing in Des Moines, Iowa, must work the "core hours" from 10:00 A.M. to 3:00 P.M. Aside from this requirement, they may set their own schedules, as long as they work the required number of hours between the hours of 6:00 A.M. and 6:00 P.M.

———

Japanese computer electronics manufacturer Matsushita created a research lab for twenty of its scientists, who are given complete freedom to pursue any projects they desire independent of the company's commercial objectives.

———

At Adobe Systems, the world's third-largest producer of personal computer software, employees set their own hours, are eligible for stock options and sabbaticals, and have access to an average of 2.5 computers. Says Charles Geschke, cofounder of the Mountain View, California, company, "Every capital asset that we have at Adobe gets into an automobile and drives home at night. Without them, there is nothing of substance in this company."

———

SUGGESTION BOX

Give higher-performing employees an opportunity to:

☞ Control budgets and resources.

☞ Access information.

☞ Communicate with others in the organization.

☞ Telecommute.

☞ Select their next assignments.

Inspiring Innovation

In his book *Getting Employees to Fall in Love With Your Company*, Jim Harris suggests four key strategies to inspire employees to act.

1. Allow the freedom to fail and try again.

2. Create freedom from bureaucracy.

3. Encourage challenges to the status quo.

4. Give everyone input into firing troublesome customers.

Compaq Computer founders Rod Canion and Jim Harris have instituted a system of decision making known as "consensus management," which relies on the skills, experience, and participation of many individuals throughout the organization rather than just a few at the very top. Apparently the system works quite well for the Houston-based company. According to Canion, "In our culture, consensus is a management tool for reaching better decisions than you would have reached on your own."

———

At the Toledo, Ohio, plant of automotive parts maker Dana Corporation, employees are allowed to spend $500 per project to improve efficiencies, without management approval. More than 80 percent of the improvements are made without the plant manager's even knowing about them in advance.

———

To encourage action, unleash energy, and minimize the stifling effects of bureaucracy, throughout his 215,000-employee international conglomerate, CEO Percy Barnevik of ABB Asea Brown Boveri, Ltd. in Zurich, Switzerland, created 5,000 separate "profit centers," each with its own profit sheet. At the same time, he shrank headquarters staff to 10 percent of its original size. Because the profit centers have, on average, no more than 50 employees, they get the advantages of working for a small business —increased responsibility, authority, and recognition. But they also have the security of working for a very large and diversified organization, as well as all its resources.

———

The Swiss Zurich Insurance group gets its employees to participate and collaborate by following these three strategies:

1. Create a small-business atmosphere.

2. Decentralize decision making as much as possible.

3. Become more customer-centered by developing expertise in customers' business.

———

FedEx, the overnight shipper, headquartered in Memphis, Tennessee, has a unique outlook on the manager-worker relationship. Says systems manager Ahmad Jaffrey, "It is our belief that the manager works for employees, not the other way around. I don't want authority. I want the job to get done."

———

Employees are energized when they are given the authority to hire their own co-workers. Candidates for permanent employment at Columbus, Ohio-based steel processor Worthington Industries must be approved by a majority of company employees before being offered a position.

———

> ❝You have to organize things such that people have the authority to do their jobs. But you need enough control to understand what's going on.❞
>
> FRANK V. CAHOUET
> Chairman,
> Mellon Bank Corporation

CASE STUDY:
XEROX LOOKS TOWARD 2000

Xerox Corporation, the leading photocopier and electronic business systems manufacturer, with more than $17 billion in annual revenues, has made some big changes over the past two decades. The changes in management's approach were necessary because of the sorry state of affairs the company found itself in in the early 1980s.

At their annual shareholders meeting in 1981, then-CEO David Kearns took questions from the audience. Assembly-line worker Frank Enos stepped up to the microphone and asked about the recently discontinued 3300 copier—a machine notoriously low in quality and reliability. Enos said, "We all know the 3300 was a piece of junk. We could've told you. Why didn't you ask us?" Although Kearns was embarrassed by the question (one he had no good answer to) at that moment he knew that something had to be done to turn things around—and quickly.

Kearns's solution was to institute an extensive program of "quality training." "What made the difference with this quality program was that it was top-down," says worker Lou Marth. "It started at the very top with Kearns.

He taught his 'family,' the people who worked for him. Then they taught those who worked for them, and it cascaded down. It took a year and a half to complete that cascading process, but everybody went through the experience—we did it worldwide with all of our employees."

During the training, employees learned all manner of things, including statistical methods, problem-solving techniques, and group process dynamics. More than 100,000 employees attended the classes, which cost the company $125 million. But the money was well spent. In 1989, Xerox received the Malcolm Baldrige Quality Award. And Frank Enos, whose challenging question had brought about Kearns's moment of truth, attended the award ceremony as Kearns's personal guest.

Looking Ahead

Xerox is not one to rest on its laurels. It's currently undertaking a major transformation of its business to respond to a changing marketplace and workforce. The program—dubbed Xerox 2000—has three key goals:

■ Transform Xerox from a command-and-control hierarchy to a more democratic organization in which employees are free to network and share their ideas with each other regardless of their rank.

■ Move from a vertical, functional orientation to a horizontal, business-process orientation.

■ Change Xerox's emphasis on always doing things better, faster, and cheaper, to a reexamination of what should be done fundamentally differently—or not at all.

While technological leadership, manufacturing might, and the production of quality products remain important parts of the equation, Xerox's current chairman and CEO, Paul A. Allaire, believes "Our future depends on our ability to motivate and lead our people to create a new kind of productivity."

Employee Power

A llaire's plan to unleash the creativity of Xerox employees—a classic model of employee empowerment—consists of five steps:

1. Break up the bureaucracy by removing layers of management, streamlining processes, and pushing decision making, responsibility, and accountability onto the employees closest to the problems.

2. Leverage diversity of race, religion, gender, and ideas, and turn it into a competitive advantage.

3. Build communities of practice—small, self-managing, entrepreneurial units where employees have the freedom to act, the security to be bold, the motivation to succeed, and the opportunity to contribute.

4. Build an organization where learning is pervasive and where failures are seen as learning opportunities, successes are studied for possible improvements, and new ideas are cherished, nurtured, and implemented.

5. Enhance the use of information technology to get employees the right information at the right time.

At Xerox, many employees now manage themselves. Time clocks are out and teams are in. Says assembler and tester Edith Page, "We are on the trust system. You know what your schedule is. We're being treated like people who are responsible enough to come and do their jobs well and then go home."

> **❝I think our story proves there's absolutely no limit to what plain, ordinary, working people can accomplish if they're given the opportunity and encouragement to do their best.❞**
>
> SAM WALTON
> Founder, Wal-Mart

Corporate law firm Morrison & Foerster in San Francisco makes it clear to its employees that everyone—regardless of their position—is important and is valued by the firm. New partners in the firm receive a handbook which reads in part, "We care about our legal assistants and staff employees. Partners are judged by their partners on how they treat people who cannot necessarily advance their careers. We do not tolerate abuse of our employees by partners, no matter how senior or how 'important.' "

When Ken Iverson took the reins at Nucor, a steel producer located in Charlotte, North Carolina, there were white hard hats for workers, blue for foremen, and green for department heads. Iverson replaced them with one color for everyone: green. As for the "executive dining room," it's the delicatessen across the street from corporate headquarters.

Software developer SAS Institute, of Cary, North Carolina, allowed employees in the company's video production department to develop a profitable, new market for the company by selling their services to outside parties. Now, almost half of the video work done in the SAS studios is for outside customers, and SAS Institute boasts the largest video production facility between Washington D.C. and Atlanta.

Organizational Flexibility

While organizations should always be on the lookout for new ways to cut costs or increase production, they should also ensure that employees have a chance to take regular breaks from the relentless pace of business. The faster an organization operates, and the harder its employees work, the more important it is for managers to allow them some flexibility. It takes happy, energized employees to make happy, energized customers. An annual picnic isn't enough.

A recent survey by Robert Half International, an employee placement company in Menlo Park, California, found that 76 percent of workers polled would leave the career fast-track in exchange for a more flexible schedule. Even more surprising, almost 66 percent said they would take a cut in pay in exchange for more flexibility.

The good news is that today approximately 42 percent of employers do offer some form of flexible scheduling, such as job-sharing or a compressed work week, to their employees. And these companies are discovering that far from negatively impacting the bottom line, these policies are increasing profits as well as employee satisfaction.

Spice-maker McCormick & Company of Hunt Valley, Maryland, has a long history of concern for its employees' needs. In 1932, when Charles P. McCormick took over the unprofitable firm from his uncle, he abolished time clocks, cut work hours from 56 to 45 a week, increased wages by 10 percent, and involved employees

> **"My job is removing obstacles and challenging people's imaginations."**
>
> —LEON ROYER
> SMS Project Manager, 3M

Bob's List

Former Labor Secretary Robert Reich credits employee involvement with making companies unique and successful. Reich cites five workplace policies as having the greatest positive effect:

1. Worker participation.

2. On-the-job training.

3. Profit sharing.

4. Flexible work rules.

5. A healthy and safe work environment.

in company decision making. McCormick was also one of the first companies to offer medical and life insurance and profit sharing. Within a year after McCormick took over, the firm became profitable, as it has remained ever since.

Hi-Tech Hose, a flexible hose and ducting products maker in Newburyport, Massachusetts, lumps all vacation time, holidays, and sick days into a single account. Employees can take time off whenever they need it and for whatever personal reasons. Employees find it energizing to be treated as responsible adults who can manage their away-from-work time.

While most large American companies now perform drug testing on their employees, Marquette Electronics of Milwaukee, Wisconsin, does not, preferring to trust its staff. When client DuPont notified Marquette that it would have to test its employees for drugs if it wanted to continue to do business with DuPont, Marquette declined. DuPont dropped the issue.

To help make its employees' commutes a little bit easier to bear, United Airlines recently set up satellite offices in the suburbs outside of San Francisco, Los Angeles, Indianapolis, and its headquarters in Chicago.

Before turning to the outside market, managers at Pitney Bowes, an office machinery manufacturer headquartered in Stamford, Connecticut, are required to consider employees in the displaced-persons program—a pool of employees whose jobs have been eliminated.

When Seattle-based outdoor equipment manufacturer REI conducted a survey to determine the best place to build a new distribution center, Salt Lake City was the best choice based on the cost savings that could be realized in a more central location. However, after REI considered the disruption that such a major move would cause its employees, it opted instead to build the new center 10 miles south of Seattle. While REI lost the benefit of $1 million in freight and shipping savings in the first year alone, it demonstrated its commitment to its employees.

When tough times require management at Atlanta-based Delta Airlines to consider cutting employee pay, top managers cut their own pay first.

American Steel & Wire Corporation in Cuyahoga Heights, Ohio, has established an employee council to review complaints about managers' decisions. The council has upheld the decisions in about half of the cases.

SUGGESTION BOX

☞ Allow employees to deviate from policy, when warranted by the circumstances.

☞ Make every effort to accommodate flexible and nontraditional work schedules.

☞ Encourage employees to have fun at work and play.

Building Flexibility and Initiative

Inc. magazine listed eight ways to encourage flexibility and individual initiative in your work force:

1. Hire slowly and fire quickly.

2. Hire people who are better or smarter than you.

3. Have a plan for identifying and easing out "toxic" employees.

4. Communicate clearly, consistently, and often.

5. Meet the people.

6. Listen, ask.

7. Give feedback.

8. Be fair.

The Erie Bolt Corporation in Erie, Pennsylvania, lets employees bid on jobs that they would normally contract to outside firms. Now, Erie Bolt's snowplowing is performed by the president of the union, and three employees and a retiree are contracted to clean and maintain the shop and equipment.

———

Advanced Micro Devices (AMD) in Sunnyvale, California, refrains from laying off employees unless the company's viability is at stake. As a demonstration of this commitment to its employees, the computer microprocessor designer and manufacturer spent $1 million to retrain 300 displaced workers. And instead of treating laid-off employees like social outcasts, as many firms do, AMD encourages them to come into the office to use company telephones, type their resumes, undergo career counseling, or engage in any number of other job-hunting activities at company expense.

———

In recognition of the importance of personal time for employee well-being, San Francisco-based corporate law firm Morrison & Foerster expects its lawyers to bill 1,800 hours a year, or approximately 36 hours a week. This compares to an average of about 2,400 a year, or more than 46 hours a week, at most major law firms. This allows the firm's lawyers to spend more time with their families and friends.

———

Ventura, California, outdoor-clothing maker Patagonia encourages its employees to take time away from the office to pursue outdoor activities. In a speech to employees, founder Yvon Chouinard said, "You are allowed to take time off, whether it's two hours or two weeks, as long as your work gets done and you don't keep others from doing their work."

> **66**The most important thing I learned from big companies is that creativity gets stifled when everyone's got to follow the rules.**99**
>
> DAVID M. KELLEY
> Founder, IDEO Product Development

Dodgeville, Wisconsin-based mail-order firm Lands' End has a unique system for filling job openings and allowing employees to find a career path that's right for them. The company encourages employees to express an interest in any department that they might want to consider moving to. Betty Bussan, who got her job in the training department through this system, explains how it works: "You can sign up for any other department. If you have an interest in seeing what packing's all about, you fill out a job enrollment form, and after a certain period of time, you get to go over there for maybe a two- or four-week period. And if it works out for you, and if it works out for the department, you can transfer there."

Instead of the businesslike uniforms required by most airlines, Dallas-based Southwest Airlines allows its employees to wear casual clothes. It is not uncommon for flight attendants and ticket agents to wear golf shirts, shorts, and sneakers—all with corporate logos.

Nordstrom Rules
———

Rule #1: Use your good judgment in all situations.

There will be no additional rules.

Please feel free to ask your department manager, store manager, or division general manager any question at any time.

At Charlotte, North Carolina's Duke Power Company, workers who are dissatisfied with their jobs can post a message on the company's electronic bulletin board. If another employee with comparable pay and work skills wants the job, the two employees can, with their supervisors' approval, swap jobs.

———

To keep employees energized by giving them new opportunities and work experiences, Epson Computers in Torrance, California, rotates them in and out of key positions. In a recent year, 29 percent of Epson's employees switched jobs within the company.

———

While there is no denying the tremendous pressure placed on employees to continue to push the edges of technology at computer software maker Microsoft, management encourages employees to find creative outlets to release the inevitable tension that is generated. Says manager Sue Boeschen, "We put sod on the floor of a colleague's office not too long ago, with a sprinkler system and lawn mowers. This would not be condoned in most companies, because we stole them from the gardener's shed. This kind of thing goes on a lot. It's not that the company encourages misbehavior, but there is a sense of fun, and playfulness, that really balances the intensity of the work."

———

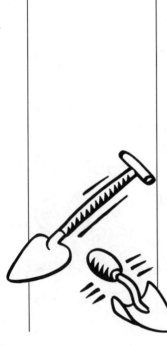

Organizational Communication

A t the organizational level, much can be done to foster communication and the spreading of information among employees. Whether through company newsletters, video conferences, taped news broadcasts, innovative question-and-answer or discussion sessions, or other forms of media, the goal is to energize employees by getting them the information they need quickly and efficiently.

A t Milwaukee, Wisconsin-based Marquette Electronics, top management is committed to energizing employees. The introduction to Marquette's employee handbook sets the tone for the company:

A NOTE FROM THE PRESIDENT

From the time we're old enough to go to school we're taught that play is fun and work is not; that we must tolerate this unpleasantness to enjoy the pleasures of life.

I never did believe that work had to be drudgery. I never felt that people should do things they're not good at or don't like to do just to make a living.

I'm convinced that a company like ours can be operated in such a way as to create an atmosphere for maximum productivity and

> **There is no 'us' and 'them' attitude here; everyone is important. Upper management is visible and accessible. There is always time to talk, to find solutions and to implement changes.**
>
> ANDREA NIEMAN,
> Administrative Assistant,
> ROLM Corporation

SUGGESTION BOX

☞ Check frequently with employees to see if the information being communicated to them is what they need and want.

☞ Be open to new and better ways of communicating with employees. For example, if you've never done a newsletter or an e-mail memo, try it.

☞ Make sure you have active ways to listen to employees, not just ways to provide them information.

creativity. I'm convinced that pleasant surroundings, good working conditions, and the lack of petty rules and regulations will bring about the greatest rewards for employee and company alike.

So Marquette tries hard to provide an atmosphere of this kind. You can see it everywhere in our new building. There are no time clocks because we assume you are honest. When you want to call home you don't have to use a pay phone; there are phones everywhere for local calls. We don't tell you what to wear, we just want you to do a good job. If you're unsuited for what you're doing, we will try to get you into something you're good at.

We strive to avoid hierarchy and organizational charts, although, obviously, there has to be some chain of command. But if you want to talk to me or any other "boss" feel free to do so. Communication is a byword we'd like very much to preserve.

I think you'll enjoy working here at Marquette.

Sincerely,
Michael J. Cudahy

Wal-Mart distribution center manager Karl Mace encourages his managers to wear jeans at least once a week so they can pitch in and help their employees with their jobs. This promotes "solidarity" and opens up channels of communication between workers and managers.

At New Hope Communications in Boulder, Colorado, a questionnaire included with every paycheck asked employees for feedback in four key areas: the employees' happiness or unhappiness with their financial package; their feelings toward other employees; their feelings about the skills they are developing; and their overall feelings about their job.

———

Goodyear Tire & Rubber, headquartered in Akron, Ohio, believes that the best route to employee empowerment is providing them with good information—and plenty of it. At Goodyear:

■ All workers can access computer files providing information about themselves, their department, and their plant.

■ Each shift tracks its own productivity. The results are posted on marker boards displayed on the shop floor and updated frequently.

■ A video network installed in each plant broadcasts training programs, employee interviews, daily announcements, and other programming of interest to employees.

■ Employee work teams meet twice each month to discuss safety, production improvements, and other issues.

■ A weekly plant newsletter is sent to each employee's home.

66Feedback is the breakfast of champions.**99**

RICK TATE
Business Consultant

Creating Partnerships

In his book *Getting Employees to Fall in Love With Your Company*, Jim Harris suggests five ways for companies to create powerful partnerships with employees:

1. Eliminate status barriers.

2. Open the company books.

3. Pay for performance, not titles.

4. Share the bad times as well as the good times.

5. Serve the frontline partners first.

At PCs Compleat, a mail-order computer retailer in Marlborough, Massachusetts, all employees are allowed to log on to the company's sales tracking system to see how well the sales force is doing. Says sales vice president Jack Littman-Quinn, "We believe if people have an awareness of sales and their part in making them, they work better and the company works better."

Enterprise Rent-A-Car, headquartered in St. Louis, Missouri, encourages friendly rivalry between its branch offices by posting the financial results of every branch office and region in plain view of all employees. This rivalry translates into energized employees who want to perform at their best at all times. New Jersey manager Woody Erhardt holds his fingers an inch apart and says, "We're this close to beating out Middlesex." He continues, "If they lose, they have to throw a party for us, and we get to decide what they wear."

At the insurance company LifeUSA in Minneapolis, Minnesota, e-mail is out and voice mail is in. Why? According to president Maggie Hughes, "It creates more personal relationships. You can listen to the voices. E-mail can be isolating. Voice mail helps people share information without becoming isolated." And Hughes should know. Every day she gets 300 to 400 voice-mail messages. Company-wide, the staff of 400 sends more than 200,000 voice-mail messages a month.

Tandem Computers in Cupertino, California, has three classes of e-mail: first-class is all business, second-class is for ideas or suggestions, and no-class is for employees to post jokes or classified ads.

An organization that is connected has a lot of power and energy. At London-based human rights organization Amnesty International, e-mail, telephone, fax, and Telex systems link some 50,000 volunteers worldwide through the organization's Urgent Action Network. When a campaign goes full swing, this network is mobilized to get the word out worldwide.

Management at the Saturn automobile factory in Spring Hill, Tennessee, understands that some employees are reluctant to tell management what is really on their minds. They developed a special electronic mail system that allows any worker to send anonymous messages to upper management and receive timely responses.

To gather information from the frontline, United Airlines president John Edwardson works with company cleaning crews and baggage handlers once a month. For many years, cleaning crews had complained about having to clean aircraft ashtrays, which are now obsolete with the prohibition of smoking on all domestic flights. After Edwardson had to dig a wad of chewing tobacco out of an ashtray with his fingers on

> "Nothing tops the question a woman asked me during the 1986 industry downturn at our open forum in Phoenix. Sitting in the front row, she asked, 'Isn't it time for Intel to change its management?' All of a sudden I had 400 people staring at me and sitting on the edges of their seats waiting for my answer. Facing those kinds of questions has honed my managerial capabilities as well as kept me reasonably humble. Intel will always be an open company, with a strong flow of information in every direction."
>
> ANDREW GROVE
> President and CEO,
> Intel Corporation

66If you want to know what's really going on in most companies, you talk to the guy who sweeps the floors. Nine times out of ten, he knows more than the president.**99**

KENNETH A. HENDRICKS
CEO, ABC Supply
Company

one of his monthly information-gathering missions with a cleaning crew, the ashtrays on all United aircraft were quickly soldered shut—once and for all.

Every weekday morning, the Ford Communications Network (FCN) broadcasts a half-hour news program to the Ford Motor Company's 360 factories and offices, and 200,000 or so viewers. Management wants employees to rely on FCN as a source of credible, timely information. Whether the news about the company is good or bad, says FCN News's executive producer, Sara Tatchio, "We want them to see it first on FCN."

At Holland, Michigan-based automobile parts manufacturer Donnelly Corporation, management displayed huge posters throughout all its plants, listing ten questions that *all* employees are encouraged to ask themselves, their colleagues, and their bosses. The questions include: "What made you mad today?" "What took too long?" "What caused complaints?" "What was misunderstood?" "What cost too much?" "What was wasted?" "What was too complicated?" "What is just plain silly?" "What took too many people?" "What job involved too many actions?" The answers to these questions can lead to employee-initiated breakthroughs in communication, improved efficiency, and cost savings.

B read Loaf Construction in Middlebury, Vermont, has a two-part system to help get employees on board with the company two different ways. First it helps employees create personal mission statements. It then holds discussions with each employee as to how he or she might integrate his or her personal missions with that of the company.

———

W hen employees are given access to company secrets, they are energized by the high level of trust that their employer has shown in them. Every employee of health-food chain Whole Foods, headquartered in Austin, Texas, has complete access to the company's financial information, including store sales, profit margins, and employee salaries. Due to the sensitivity of this information, the company's 6,500 employees have all been designated as "insiders" for stock-trading by the SEC.

———

A t Buckman Laboratory's manufacturing plant in Ghent, Belgium, walkie-talkies purchased to allow one department to contact another without disturbing any other departments were found to be defective—they picked up communications from all departments. However, when the management of the specialty chemical company noticed that employees using the "defective" equipment were becoming much more involved and offering solutions to problems in other departments, they didn't bother to get them fixed.

———

In his book *Post-Capitalist Society*, management expert Peter Drucker states that each employee has to be asked:

❝'What should we hold *you* accountable for?' 'What information do *you* need?' and, in turn, 'What information do *you* owe the rest of us?' . . . Each worker has to be a participant in decisions as to what equipment is needed; how the work should be scheduled; indeed, what the basic policy of the entire company should be.❞

66 In the industrial age, the CEO sat on the top of the hierarchy and didn't really have to listen to anybody. . . . In the information age, you have to listen to the ideas of people regardless of where they are in the organization. **99**

JOHN SCULLEY
Former CEO, Apple
Computer Co.

ABL Electronics of Timonium, Maryland, takes employees off the assembly plant floor and on field trips to show them how the company's products are used. Stops include hospitals where their products are used in fetal monitoring devices. Not only do employees have a better understanding of how the company's products are used, but they take more pride in their work.

———

An employee stood up in a Diesel Technology Corporation meeting and announced that he had been making plungers for 15 years, and had no idea whatsoever how they fit into the company's product. Derek Kaufman, president of the Wyoming, Michigan, manufacturer of fuel injectors, challenged any employee who was interested to try to assemble an injector on his or her own. To facilitate the process, Kaufman and a few staff members disassembled 50 fuel injectors. Of the company's 550 employees, 505 took the challenge. As a result, some 90 percent of the employees—including janitors, secretaries, accountants, production workers, and management—earned "I Got It Together" T-shirts.

———

Employees who are kept informed about the financial health of their company are energized by management's concern for their needs. Every Wal-Mart store and warehouse broadcasts the closing price of the company's stock each day over the intercom and associates receive detailed information on their stores' weekly sales and profit numbers.

———

Every month, managers at Environmental Compliance Services, an environmental insurance firm in Exton, Pennsylvania, chart the performance of each of the company's profit centers and post the results on bulletin boards for all employees to see. The result is not only more competition, but more cooperation among teams. When one department is in a slump, employees in other departments jump in to help out.

After a round of painful layoffs, management at Patagonia, a manufacturer of outdoor clothing in Ventura, California, opened its books to employees so they would understand why costs had to be reduced. Workers appreciated management's efforts to inform them and they responded by helping managers make substantial cost cuts.

The monthly internal newsletter of FedEx, an overnight shipper headquartered in Memphis, Tennessee, has two regular columns devoted to keeping employees updated on what competitors such as UPS and the U.S. Postal Service are up to. Employee surveys show that these are among the most popular items in the newsletter.

Many companies energize their employees and improve service to their customers by facilitating direct communication between the employees who do the work and the consumer.

Handling Transitions

Change is a part of business today, but employees are often afraid of how major company changes will affect them. Here are 10 ways to help your employees deal with transitions:

1. Communicate, communicate, communicate.

2. Adopt a positive attitude.

3. Share your excitement about the change with everyone you meet.

4. Involve employees in making decisions that affect them and their work.

5. Change only what needs to be changed.

6. Be honest and timely with good news *and* with bad.

7. Be clear and consistent about your expectations.

8. Don't surprise your employees.

9. Once the process is started, don't hesitate to follow through.

10. Fight false rumors with truth and information.

❝Interoffice mail. E-mail. Voice mail. Whatever happened to face-mail?❞

Advertisement for Steelcase office furniture

At Carbide Surface of Frasier, Michigan, customers can deal directly with the employees who do the work. If a customer needs a tool coated with carbide, he is referred to one of the "impregnators" who do the coating. Customers like the system because it results in a product that more closely resembles customer needs. Employees like the interaction because it challenges them and makes their jobs more interesting.

Goodyear Tire and Rubber in Akron, Ohio, uses computer networks to provide information to its employees. Says vice president Frederick Kovac, "It used to be, if you wanted information, you had to go up, over, and down through the organization. Now you just tap in."

In an energized organization, open communication starts at the top. William Duff, president of FormPac of Sandusky, Ohio, was concerned that because employees were unaware of the company's financials, they might not fully understand how company resources were being utilized. To rectify the situation, Duff began posting the plastic packaging company's monthly sales and pretax profits on a display board near the time clock, along with industry reports indicating the state of the company's markets.

Twice a year, employees at clothing manufacturer Levi Strauss, headquartered in San

Francisco, rate their supervisors and co-workers on factors such as communicating effectively, promoting teamwork and trust, and empowering others.

———

Instead of the usual supervisor-led performance evaluations, employees at Computer Specialists in Rockville, Maryland, are asked to rate their own performance, and clients are asked to rate worker performance twice a year. After each rating, the company president meets with each employee to compare the two evaluations and to discuss successes as well as needed improvements.

———

General Electric, which is headquartered in Fairfield, Connecticut, employs "360-degree" employee evaluations, with input from peers and subordinates, as well as superiors. According to CEO Jack Welch, "These are the roughest evaluations anyone can get; people hear things about themselves they've never heard before. But they get the input they need, and the chance to improve."

———

At the Nissan automobile manufacturing plant in Newcastle, England, employees rate their own performance at the same time their supervisors are rating them. Afterward, they get together to compare results and discuss the areas where employees are doing well, as well as where there is a need for improvement.

———

> **"**Be guided by the axiom: There are no limits to the ability to contribute on the part of a properly selected, well-trained, appropriately supported, and, above all, committed person.**"**
>
> —TOM PETERS
> *Thriving On Chaos*

CASE STUDY:
SRC CORPORATION OPENS ITS BOOKS

One of the latest and most successful ways to improve the bottom line is known as open-book management—teaching employees how to understand the company's "numbers," and their role in improving performance. And one of the most successful practitioners of open-book management is SRC Corporation, an engine rebuilder in Springfield, Missouri.

Not only was SRC's President and CEO Jack Stack one of the first practitioners of open-book management, but he was one of the first business leaders to be able to demonstrate the compelling financial benefits of the practice.

The "Great Game of Business" —Stack's name for his visionary open-book management—has its roots in Stack's years at International Harvester in Melrose Park, Illinois. At age 26, Stack was assigned to run the machining division, which was ranked dead last in productivity. Stack's idea was unique: he gave his foremen daily productivity statistics for the division—broken down by each of the foremen—and then compared their performance to that of other plant divisions. It didn't take long for the division's productivity to climb. Only three months after Stack started opening up the books, the division went from last place to first in the plant's productivity ratings.

Numbers Talk

Impressed with Stack's results, International Harvester assigned him to its remanufacturing divisions in Springfield, Missouri—a plant that lost $2 million in the year before Stack started there. Harvester gave Stack six months to decide whether the plant should be shut down.

To get things back on track, Stack chose three goals—product quality, housekeeping, and safety. When the plant went 100,000 hours without an accident, Stack closed it down for a day and held a monumental beer bust, complete with a parade of forklift trucks decorated with crepe paper, and fire extinguisher-toting employees marching to the theme song from *Rocky* blasting over the plant's loudspeakers. Soon, Stack's departments regularly exceeded their production goals and, within nine months, the plant had made a $250,000 profit.

In the more than 15 years since Stack's arrival at SRC, sales have grown from about $26 million to more than $100 million a year. Not only that, but many other companies have jumped onto the open-book management bandwagon, including Sprint's government systems divisions, Amoco Canada, and the 50,000-employee ZCCM copper mine in Zambia. And every month, some 30 to 35 companies attend SRC's Great Game of Business two-day training program. It is an investment that pays off. Within two years after adopting open-book management policies, for example Mid-States Technical, a staffing company in Davenport, Iowa, increased its revenues by 79 percent.

> **"I needed to teach anyone who moved a broom or operated a grinder everything the bank knew. That way they could really understand how every nickel saved could make a difference."**
>
> JACK STACK,
> President and CEO

How It Works

SRC practices three basic tenets of open-book management:

■ Every employee sees—and learns to understand—the company's financials, along with all the other numbers that are critical to tracking the business's performance. Numbers, ratios, charts, and graphs are distributed or posted anywhere and everywhere possible to ensure that employees have full access to them. However, the numbers aren't worth the paper they're printed on if employees can't understand them. Open-book companies therefore train their employees to understand the numbers, to compare projections with actual results and to understand whether the company is making money, losing money, or just maintaining the status quo.

■ Employees learn that, whatever else they do, part of their job is to move those numbers in the right direction. Every employee—from the president on down to the entry-level clerk or laborer—has a part in helping the company make its numbers. Employees are taught how to track their performance against the company's goals. Every employee is accountable to every other employee for maintaining his or her performance.

■ Employees have a direct stake in the company's success. If the company is

Continued on next page.

profitable, the employees get a piece of it. If the company isn't profitable, there is nothing for them to share in. When employees are rewarded for helping to make the company profitable, they will do whatever they can to make it happen.

"All companies play the same game," Stack observes. "We all have to determine the same sets of numbers. It's just that in most companies so few people know the numbers. The message the CEO gives to the investors at the end of the year is impersonal and has nothing to do with all the things the workers did. And then people talk about creating job security. The only measurement of job security is in the balance sheet."

The Proof Is in the Pudding

Do employees working under the open-book system of management really know so much more about their companies than workers at traditionally managed firms? At SRC they certainly do. When Bill Fotsch was working for the farm-machinery manufacturer Case Corporation, he flew to Missouri to visit SRC, one of Case's vendors. Fotsch had been told that SRC employees knew a lot about their business, so he decided to put it to the test.

While on a tour of the plant, Fotsch asked a worker who was polishing crankshaft journals if he knew the price of the crankshaft he was working on. Fotsch didn't expect the SRC employee to know the difference between the terms "cost" and "price," much less the *actual* price of the part. But to his surprise, the unruffled worker asked, "List price or dealer net?" He then proceeded to name both prices, as well as what it cost SRC to manufacture the crankshaft, and his part of that cost. According to Fotsch, he became a convert to SRC's open-book management program on the spot. He now works as a business advisor to Stack.

Because Stack's employees are not only knowledgeable about the business, but have a direct stake in its success, they are always on the lookout for ways to improve operations. Over a two-year period, engine disassembler Freeman Tracy saved SRC approximately $2 million with the 88 different suggestions he submitted for approval. And since SRC pays its employees up to $500 for each idea submitted, Tracy made $10,000 for his efforts. Charles Albright, an engine assembler, says, "The thing that motivates me is knowing the company is looking out for me; so I am going to look out for them. That's the bottom line for me."

Daily production status meetings at the Allied Signal Industrial Fibers plant in Moncure, North Carolina, were extremely divisive and confrontational until managers started making an effort to catch each other "doing things right." Now, instead of blaming each other for problems the department heads make a point of praising each other's successes, and the meetings have changed from a confrontational win/lose atmosphere to a cooperative win/win one.

> **Go to the people. Learn from them. Love them. Start with what they know. Build on what they have. But of the best leaders, when their task is accomplished, their work is done, the people will remark: We have done it ourselves.**
>
> Lao-Tse saying

———

Whenever Vancouver City Savings Credit Union in British Columbia experiences a major operational change, management develops a staff forum as part of the change management process. For the 32 branches in the Vancouver metropolitan area, it's a golden opportunity for employees to gather together, communicate face to face, and address whatever concerns they might have. Each forum has a theme; a recent one was named "Mission Possible," with executives dressed as secret agents whose mission was to deliver a new approach to selling. Another forum involved a "journey" to new methods of financial services called "Relationship Building." According to Lauren St. John, manager of employee development, "Staff packed their bags with brand new ideas, threw out old ones, and got on the road to move toward a new way of doing things."

———

Mark Taylor, CEO of AFS Window and Door Corporation in Anaheim, California, puts

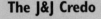

The J&J Credo

The Johnson & Johnson credo sets the tone for how the company and those who work for it are expected to act. The paragraph pertaining to the treatment of employees is a model that any business should be proud to emulate:

"We are responsible to our employees, the men and women who work with us throughout the world. Everyone must be considered as an individual. We must respect their dignity and recognize their merit. They must have a sense of security in their jobs. Compensation must be fair and adequate, and working conditions clean, orderly, and safe. We must be mindful of ways to help our employees fulfill their family responsibilities. Employees must feel free to make suggestions and complaints. There must be equal opportunity for employment, development, and advancement for those qualified. We must provide competent management, and their actions must be just and ethical."

a positive spin on the need for employees to improve their work practices by holding a special meeting with his employees every other month. He serves pizza as the employees watch videos of actual customers at construction sites, pointing out problems they've had with the company's windows. Since instituting the meetings, customer complaints have decreased 60 percent and returns due to poor shipping and handling have virtually disappeared.

Management at the Queen Mary resort in Long Beach, California, holds monthly meetings with line employees to brainstorm ideas on how the company can improve their jobs. An employee committee then votes on which ideas are the best and would be easiest to implement. The result is involved, motivated, and energized employees.

Wilson Sculley Associates, an advertising agency in St. Louis, Missouri, conducts Saturday morning QUIT (QUarterly Internal Talk) meetings to show all employees the same company data and plans that are presented to the company's board of directors. Employees are energized by the meetings, and company billings rose from $8.8 to $15 million in a single year.

Chocolate maker Hershey Foods of Hershey, Pennsylvania, has instituted a program to encourage worker participation and teamwork called Quality Through Excellence. Along with this program, the company has made significant efforts to improve communication between all employees throughout the organization—primarily by holding regular meetings where employees can ask plant managers or department heads frank questions in an open and safe environment. According to employees, the meetings have been clearly energizing. Says chocolate paste processor Donald Hainly, "I think it's great. It used to be they wouldn't tell you anything. Now, if they are putting in a new production line, a lot of times they will come and ask for suggestions, instead of putting it in and then making all the changes after it's already there."

To ensure that communication occurs frequently and freely between company managers, at Advanced Micro Devices in Sunnydale, California, CEO Jerry Sanders sponsors a quarterly "Breakfast with Jerry" at the company's main manufacturing facilities in California and Texas. During these breakfasts—attended by all of the computer microprocessor manufacturer's managers—Sanders discusses where the company has been, where it is going, and then opens the floor for questions. The managers feel involved in the inner workings of the company and are energized as a result.

All monthly officers' and directors' meetings at Herman Miller, an office furniture designer and manufacturer in Zeeland, Michigan,

Shake It Up

Employees in any company can become complacent. In his book *Leading Change,* John P. Kotter suggests the following six ways to shake up the status quo:

1. Create a crisis by allowing a financial loss to occur or an error to blow up.

2. Eliminate obvious excess like corporate jet fleets and executive dining rooms.

3. Set targets for income, productivity, and cycle time so high they can't be reached by doing business as usual.

4. Share information about customer satisfaction and financial performance with employees.

5. Insist that people talk regularly to unsatisfied customers, unhappy suppliers, and disgruntled shareholders.

6. Include honest discussion of the firm's problems in company newspapers and management speeches. Curb senior-management "happy talk."

"Continuous, supportive communication from managers, supervisors and associates is too often underemphasized. It is a major, major motivator."

JIM MOULTROP
Consultant, Management
Perspectives Group

are videotaped and distributed to its employees, building powerful connections.

———

Ben Edwards, CEO of stock brokerage A.G. Edwards and Sons in St. Louis, Missouri, conducts a nationwide speaker-phone meeting with all of his employees on the last Friday of each month. The meetings begin with a brief state-of-the-company talk; then Edwards opens the phone lines for a real-time, question-and-answer period.

———

A long-standing tradition at office equipment manufacturer Pitney Bowes in Stamford, Connecticut, is the annual jobholders' meeting. Begun in 1947, this meeting gives employees an opportunity to ask senior management any question they want. According to CEO George Harvey, "Employees can stand up and challenge management and feel good about doing it."

———

Telecommunications giant Motorola in Schaumberg, Illinois, hosts quarterly face-to-face "town meetings" with employees in which executives share the latest company news. They realize, however, that many employees may not speak up in large group settings out of apprehension or embarrassment. So, after the meeting, the executives hold follow-up "rap sessions"— break-out meetings with much smaller groups to encourage two-way interaction.

———

Tassani Communications, an advertising agency in Chicago, established a formal employee "sounding board," in which nonmanagerial employees from each department meet twice a month with the company's founder to express their needs and perspectives.

Renaissance Harborplace Hotel in Baltimore, Maryland, chartered a Quality Circle team that meets once a month to discuss opportunities for improvement throughout the hotel—everything from quality of work-life issues such as the employee cafeteria, to providing high-quality guest service. According to the hotel's training manager, Rod Bourn, "If the team *really* wants to get the attention of our more than 600 employees, they'll do a skit or make a movie to be shown at a quarterly meeting."

To keep employees up-to-date on the company's performance, management at Atmosphere Processing, an automotive supplier in Holland, Michigan, holds an annual job holders' meeting which all employees are invited to attend. At this three-hour meeting, key managers present reports on company profits, expenditures, investments, and strategies.

All employees of Overland Data, a computer peripherals manufacturer in San Diego, California, are invited to attend the weekly executive committee meeting. Every meeting includes

Gore's Governing Principles

While W.L. Gore & Associates, maker of Gore-Tex® and other high tech fabrics in Newark, Delaware, has no formal rules, the company *does* have a set of governing principles that all associates agree to abide by. They are:

1. Sincerely strive to be fair with each other, our suppliers, our customers, and all persons with whom we carry out transactions.

2. Allow, help, and encourage associates to grow in knowledge, skill, scope of responsibility, and range of activities.

3. Make your own commitments—and keep them.

4. Consult with associates before taking actions that might be "below the waterline" and cause serious damage to the enterprise.

> **"**The leader needs to be in touch with the employees and to communicate with them on a daily basis.**"**
>
> DONALD PETERSEN
> Former Chairman,
> Ford Motor Company

reports on cash position, shipments, customer service reports, and production goals. Says CFO Charlie Monts, "When a company grows 40 percent annually, there are enough changes in a single week to make a significant impact on the company." Employee attendance at these meetings ensures that *all* employees have the opportunity to be kept informed and up to date.

Employee safety is *always* the first topic discussed at every meeting at Nypro, a plastic injection molder in Clinton, Massachusetts, whether it's a meeting of the warehouse shipping staff or the company's annual banquet. As a result, Nypro cut its workers' compensation bill from $500,000 to $100,000.

Employees at Solar Press, a direct-mail company located in Naperville, Illinois, attended a one-day, off-site presentation of the company's long-range plans dubbed "Brain Day." In the morning session, employees were given presentations on the company's sales projections, production goals, new products, and the discontinuation of certain product lines as well as the consolidation of operations that would result. In the afternoon, the employees met by department to make plans for the upcoming year. Employees were energized by being included in the planning process, sales increased 18 percent for the year, and 100 new employees were added to the company's payroll.

When the British subsidiary of household product manufacturer S.C. Johnson Wax of Racine, Wisconsin, celebrated its 70th anniversary in 1984, then-CEO Samuel C. Johnson wanted to find a way to mark the occasion while opening communication between the employees of the British subsidiary and the home office. Johnson's solution was to fly the entire British staff of 480 employees to Racine for a three-day visit to headquarters and then a weekend in New York, before flying them back to Britain. When the Australian subsidiary turned 70 in 1987, all 230 employees were flown to Racine and then to Los Angeles for a weekend. And when the Canadian subsidiary had its 70th birthday in 1990, the 350 employees of Johnson Wax-Canada were also flown to Racine for a visit, and then on to Washington D.C.

High-Performance Characteristics

In its report, *The Road to High-Performance Workplaces: A Guide to Better Jobs and Better Business Results,* the Department of Labor's Office of the American Workplace identified the following characteristics of high-performance organizations:

1. Opportunity for training and continuous learning.

2. Sharing of information.

3. Employee participation.

4. Flat organizational structures.

5. Cross-level employee partnerships.

6. Compensation linked to performance.

7. Layoffs avoided at all cost.

8. Supportive work environment.

9. Integration of all of these practices into the organization's long-term strategy.

Suggestion Programs

While every organization has employees who are more than happy to make suggestions, there are also those who, because of shyness, lack of confidence, or intimidation, do not make their ideas for improvement known to their supervisors. Their ideas are no less valid than those of their more vocal co-workers—indeed, they may be even better. When First Maryland Bancorp in Baltimore, Maryland, started up its Brainstorm program—designed to motivate employees to submit cost-saving and sales-increasing ideas—the 12-week program was strictly voluntary. This didn't deter 95 percent of its 4,000-strong workforce from participating. As a result, First Maryland saved an estimated $24 million. Suggestion systems are an important way for organizations to solicit ideas from all their employees—regardless of who they are or where they are in the organization's hierarchy.

> **66**Companies don't need management stars or heroes to thrive. What they absolutely do need is an effective system for getting and implementing ideas from the people who do the work.**99**
>
> MARTIN EDELSTON,
> CEO, Boardroom, Inc.

The personal involvement, or the lack thereof, of an organization's top management is a critical factor in the success or failure of suggestion programs, and in the resulting energy level of employees who participate. Ron Kiripolsky, the former president of a 500-person division of PSA Airlines, now part of USAir, personally opened the organization's suggestion box at the beginning of each work day, read the suggestions, and met with the suggestors and their supervisors that day to discuss the suggestions and work out implementation.

At Freightliner Corporation's truck manu-facturing plant in Cleveland, North Carolina, employees are energized by "cause and effect" boards placed throughout the plant. Along with each board is a supply of both yellow and blue Post-it note pads. Any employee who has an idea about the cause of a quality-related problem is encouraged to fill out a yellow note to describe the situation and post it on the board. If an employee has a suggestion for solving a problem, he or she fills out a blue note and places it on the board in response.

When Hughes Aircraft in Los Angeles adopted its employee suggestion program, it found that certain revisions made it more successful. These included:

- Eliminating the regulation that allowed only salaried employees to participate.

- Emphasizing the value of small suggestions rather than going only for the big ones.

- Developing firm standards for qualifying and calculating savings based on these suggestions.

- Eliminating the misconception that professional people are not interested in improvement efforts.

- Increasing management understanding of and support for suggestions.

- Increasing management's understanding of the value of sincere appreciation by management and peers for ideas developed by individuals and teams.

SUGGESTION BOX

☛ Ensure that all suggestions are reviewed and acted on soon after they are submitted.

☛ Make sure you respond to, and actually try to use, as many suggestions as possible, and thank those who submitted them.

☛ Widely publicize suggestions used and their positive impact on the organization.

" How a company deals with mistakes suggests how well it will bring out the best ideas and talents of its people, and how effectively it will respond to change. When employees know that mistakes won't lead to retribution, it creates an atmosphere in which people are willing to come up with ideas and suggest changes. This is important to a company's long-term success. **"**

BILL GATES
Chairman and CEO,
Microsoft Corporation

At one time, at clothing manufacturer Levi Strauss, in San Francisco, more than $3 million was set aside for developing employee ideas for new products, and budgets of up to $500,000 were offered for some of the best ideas. Simple, two-page marketing plans were requested from participating employees.

———

Noel Goutard, CEO of French auto parts manufacturer Valeo, holds all of his employees personally responsible for making at least 10 suggestions for improvement each year. Every suggestion must be responded to within 10 days. The result is more than 25,000 energized Valeo employees, and more than 250,000 suggestions for improvement every year.

———

To re-energize the old concept of the suggestion box, Com-Corp Industries, a metal stamping company in Cleveland, Ohio, has installed "screwup boxes" to let employees tell management when they are doing something wrong. Comments, questions, and complaints are posted on the company bulletin board along with management's responses.

———

An important element in the success of any suggestion program is ensuring that employees have access to the information they need to make informed judgments. At Weslake, Ohio, building materials manufacturer Manco, charts containing key company financial data includ-

SCREW-UP
BOX

ing sales, revenue growth, and productivity are posted on the cafeteria walls. The company's salespeople conduct weekly meetings to review their territories in front of *all* employees and seek everyone's ideas and suggestions for improving client sales and service.

All employees—managers included—are energized when their advice is sought and used. Golden Apple Management Company, a fast-food restaurant operator based in Dothan, Alabama, uses management advisory councils to obtain feedback from frontline managers. Their input is then used to modify policy, procedures, or practices.

At Stew Leonards, the self-titled "world's largest dairy store" in Danbury, Connecticut, employee and customer suggestions are taken very seriously. Every day at 8:30 A.M., the suggestion box is emptied. By 10:00 A.M. all suggestions are typed up and delivered to the store's managers. And, by no later than 2:00 P.M. all suggestions are discussed in staff meetings, where managers are encouraged to find ways to implement the suggestions rather than reasons to reject them.

Personal-care products retailer, the Body Shop, is known for its progressive and unconventional management practices. Its open communication is known as the DODGI—

The Scanlon Plan

As a way to empower and energize workers and to involve them in the running of their businesses, many firms have adopted the Scanlon Plan. This program, developed in the 1940s and '50s by Joe Scanlon, a United Steelworkers of America researcher, has four principles:

1. Identity. Everyone in the company must understand the business, its goals, and the need for profitability.

2. Participation. Everyone in the company must have the opportunity to influence decisions.

3. Competence. Each person must continually improve his or her abilities.

4. Equity. Returns should be shared with employees, investors, and customers. Each must get a fair return.

> **"**The hard stuff is easy. The soft stuff is hard. And the soft stuff is a lot more important than the hard stuff.**"**
>
> DR. TOM MALONE
> President and CEO,
> Milliken & Company

Department of Darned Good Ideas. Employees of the Little Hampton, England-based company suggest ways to make things better, including how management can "ennoble their lives" and "make their spirits sing."

———

When business was down dramatically a few years ago at Lincolnshire, Illinois, benefits and compensation consultant Hewitt Associates, president Pete Friedes informed all employees of the situation in a series of detailed memos, and asked them to come forward with cost-saving ideas. And come they did! As a result of their suggestions—including ideas such as moving the FedEx delivery time from morning to afternoon, and cutting out the annual company picnic—the firm saved more than $15 million a year, as well as the jobs of all its associates and partners.

———

All Wegmans supermarkets hold a monthly employee breakfast. At these meetings, the store manager and personnel representative meet with a group of randomly selected employees to talk about problems and generate ideas and solutions. At one meeting, some cashiers mentioned how hard it was to stand on their feet all the time. The manager immediately purchased cushioned mats for them and the idea quickly spread throughout the rest of the Rochester, New York-based chain.

———

The Office of Human Resources and Administration at the U.S. Department of Energy in Washington, D.C., sponsored an "Ideas Day" for all employees to examine ways to improve customer service, streamline work processes, and enhance the workplace environment. During the week following Ideas Day, staff received 2,134 ideas, and 68 percent of them were implemented.

> 66 Once people trust management, know they're responsible, and are given the training, it's astonishing what they can do for customers and ultimately for the shareholders. 99
>
> JAMES HENDERSON
> CEO, Cummins Engine Company, Inc.

———

Sun International, a resort hotel operator headquartered in Johannesburg, South Africa, lets employees and their spouses spend a night as guests in their own hotel so they can gauge the performance of the hotel staff and provide suggestions for improvement. The employees are energized by the opportunity to spend a special night away from home, and the company benefits from their suggestions.

———

To help encourage evaluators of employee suggestions to review suggestions as quickly as possible, San Antonio, Texas, insurer USAA has instituted the "Slice of the PIE" program. PIE is an acronym for USAA's "Partners in Excellence" suggestion program. For every suggestion that is approved or disapproved, evaluators receive a paper "slice of PIE" that can be taped to their unit's poster facsimile of a pie pan. When evaluators fill their posters with eight slices of pie, they can redeem them for a brunch for their work unit.

———

> **"**To create a competitive edge in today's business world, organizations are trying to do more with fewer employees, so it's imperative that employees are rewarded for using problem-solving and decision-making skills. No activity is more important to the organization.**"**
>
> DAVID W. SMITH
> President, Action
> Management Associates

During a downturn in business, employees at Rosenbluth International, a Philadelphia-based corporate travel agency, submitted more than 400 cost-saving ideas as part of "Operation Brainstorm." As a result of these, the company was able to avoid laying off employees.

———

To help employees become better participants in company suggestion programs, Cummins Engine, the world's largest independent manufacturer of diesel engines, in Columbus, Indiana, management sends production employees to Dale Carnegie courses. Cummins has found that these courses help employees communicate better and more confidently in their work groups.

———

Employees at Com-Corp Industries, a metal stamper in Cleveland, Ohio, are required to submit a detailed review of the company's performance three times a year. This practice creates an ongoing dialogue between employees and managers, and the company gets lots of valuable suggestions for improvement in the process.

———

Jack Welch, chairman of General Electric, encouraged his employees to get involved and to champion new ideas when he reduced the corporate planning staff—and all the red tape that went along with it—by 80 percent.

———

CASE STUDY:
MAKING THE CITY OF PHOENIX NUMBER ONE

Phoenix, Arizona, has been attracting a lot of attention lately. In a 1995 international competition to recognize the best-run city government in the world, Phoenix was awarded the Carl Bertelsmann Prize. The city, which was praised for its highly efficient and consumer-oriented programs, shared the top prize of $180,000 with Christchurch, New Zealand. Phoenix was also recognized as the best-managed of the nation's 30 largest cities by *Financial World* and was the only competitor to receive a straight-A report card in the magazine's annual "State of the Cities" rankings. And in a survey of Phoenix residents, the city government earned an 81 percent approval rating.

Smart Suggestions

How did it do all this? By energizing its employees through numerous innovative programs to solicit suggestions, improve communication, create new training opportunities, and facilitate a wide array of other activities beneficial to employees.

The City of Phoenix employee suggestion program, which has received several national awards for the most dollars saved per employee among all state and local governments, is designed to encourage employees to submit ideas that promote cost savings or measurable improvements in productivity, product quality, employee morale, or safety. Suggestions eligible for cash awards include those that:

- Result in increased productivity.

- Result in documentable cost avoidance or cost savings.

- Combine operations without sacrificing quality.

- Reduce the cost of materials or supplies.

- Simplify, reduce, or eliminate paperwork and reports.

The system is well organized and efficient. Employees are notified in writing about the final disposition of their suggestions within 60 days of the date the suggestion was received. Employees may be eligible for certificates of award, certificates of commendation, plaques, or cash

Continued on next page.

awards of up to $2,500, for suggestions which are accepted. When a suggestion is rejected, a letter is sent to the employee giving a full explanation of why the idea was not adopted. Employees are allowed to appeal the decision of the Suggestion Committee for up to one year after the date of the rejection letter.

Passport to the City

In another successful program, graduates of the City of Phoenix Supervisory Academy are given the chance to become more familiar with other city departments through the "Passport to the City" program. Throughout the year, four different city department sites are showcased with site tours, discussions, informational sessions, and networking activities. Participants are issued "passports" and stamps to record their travel adventures. After adding six stamps to their passports, the supervisors receive special recognition and they network with other supervisors and employees. Says aquatic maintenance coordinator Sylvan Kinney, one of the first two travelers to receive six stamps, "I was amazed at the diversity of work city employees do.

The program gave me a greater understanding of other departments."

Another successful city initiative is the middle management rotation program, which provides middle managers with the opportunity to expand their skills while increasing interdepartmental communication and understanding. A weekly employee newsletter, *City Connection*, implemented to improve employee communications, is overseen by an editorial board with representatives from all city departments.

A Statement of Values

Another thing that helps employees all pull together is a clear statment of the organization's vision and values. Here is the City of Phoenix's statement.

■ **We are dedicated to serving our customers.** We succeed by focusing our attention on the customer. The city exists to serve the customer and our community. Their needs give us our direction and purpose. They need to feel and sense our commitment to them.

■ **We work as a team.** Teamwork is the basis of our success. We use cooperation as our first tool in working with others—employees, departments, and the private sector. We involve people because we value their commitment and ownership. We view successful performance as a group activity. There is nothing we cannot accomplish together. One unit of the city cannot be successful at the expense of another. Our team work and cooperative spirit reaches out to the customer—we include the customer in our team.

■ **We each do all we can.** We are the city's most important resource. We are committed. We each have the opportunity and responsibility to develop and use our skills to the highest level. We value diversity. To be successful, we all contribute our ideas and creativity to improving the city. We are proud of the statement our work makes about us.

■ **We learn, change, and improve.** We are open to new methods and we listen to others. We correct our mistakes and learn from them. We continually strive to be faster, smarter, and better than we were the year before.

■ **We focus on results.** Each of us knows the level of our customer satisfaction, our response time in delivering services, and the cost of those services. We use information about the results we provide so we can improve. There are times when bureaucracy is a barrier to achieving the desired result. Where rules do not add value, we want to change them to better focus on results and customer satisfaction.

■ **We work with integrity.** Whenever we make a decision, provide a service, or deal with customers, we act with honesty and integrity. People learn from interacting with us that they can continue to trust us. We treat all people equally and equitably.

■ **We work to make Phoenix better.** Improving transportation, the environment, public safety, educational opportunities, and other parts of our community is the reason we come to work each day. It's the reason we want to change and improve. Making Phoenix a better place to live and work is our bottom line. We care about our community.

Clearly, the City of Phoenix is a leader in involving employees in improving its operations *and* in opening up the lines of communication within the organization. It's a winning combination that can't be beat!

Employee Development Programs

Employee development pays important dividends for both organizations and employees. Many organizations have created comprehensive training programs to ensure that their employees have the opportunity to improve their work skills and to prepare them for advancement in the organization. While some of the programs are highly structured, others allow employees to identify their own training opportunities. In a recent study of workplace practices, it was found that companies that invest in their employees find it well worth it. According to the study:

- Firms that invest in employee development have significantly higher market values than those that don't.

- Firms that actively encourage employee development and offer opportunities for employee involvement made much larger gains in productivity than those that didn't.

- Of all the employee practices reviewed, total quality management (TQM) was the most successful. TQM is a system in which employees are trained and encouraged to be constantly on the lookout for ways to improve business processes and practices. The stock price of firms with superior TQM programs increased significantly within the five-year period after implementation of TQM. Approximately 85 percent of American firms have instituted employee involvement programs such as TQM.

To encourage young employees to consider a career in management, Winn-Dixie supermarkets, headquartered in Jacksonville, Florida, sponsor "Youth Management Day," a day when more than 800 part-time employees between the ages of 15 and 20 manage the store for the day. To prepare them for the big day, Winn-Dixie puts each youth manager through one full week of training.

———

Employee training has always been a priority at IBM, headquartered in Armonk, New York. At an early point in the organization's development, founder Thomas Watson had only one staff member—an education director.

———

Before it started operation of its new manufacturing plant in Smyrna, Tennessee, Nissan spent $63 million in training, or about $30,000 for each of its 2,000 workers, to bring them up to speed.

———

As part of trucking company Con-Way Transportation Services' "Walk a Mile in My Shoes" program, drivers and executives regularly trade jobs. On the swap days, drivers get a taste of what it's like to be a manager of the Menlo Park, California, company, and managers get to see what a driver's day is like.

———

SUGGESTION BOX

☛ Make sure every employee has a development goal—to learn a skill, take a course, etc.

☛ Make employees active participants in directing their own development opportunities.

☛ Announce opportunities available to your employees as often as possible and distribute the information as widely as possible. Use newsletters, e-mail, voice mail, presentations by human resources staff, staff meetings, and any other way you can think of to get the word out.

❝The message we give employees is that they're responsible for their career development, but we'll help them figure out which paths are the best for them to take.❞

ADELLE DIGIORGIO
Corporate Employee
Relations Director,
Apple Computer

English supermarket giant, Tesco, gives each of its employees 100 educational credits each year. Employees are allowed to use the credits to "buy" the training courses of their choice—either inside or outside of the company. As a result, employee training activity has increased dramatically.

———

By creating a partnership with employees, Pat Carrigan, manager of the General Motors assembly plant in Lakewood, Georgia, was able to bring absenteeism down from 25 percent to 9 percent in a four-year period. Her partnership included:

- A two-week orientation training program for all new employees.

- An ongoing training program that provided the 3,000 employees with approximately 360,000 hours of learning in a two-year period.

- Establishment of 133 work teams, involving 90 percent of the workforce.

———

Every three months or so, Craig Weatherup, president of PepsiCo, based in Purchase, New York, gathers together his top managers to identify the area of the company most in need of immediate improvement. He then gives himself and his staff 90 days to do two things: 1) Learn all they can about how to improve that area, and 2) train their employees in that area. The newly trained middle managers are then given 90 days

to learn all they can and to train *their* employees, and so on, throughout their worldwide operations. When the first 90-day cycle is complete, and all next-level managers have been trained, Weatherup again gathers his top managers to decide on the *next* area in need of improvement, and the training cycle continues.

———

Beaverton, Oregon-based Sequent Computer Systems assigns every new-hire a sponsor—a veteran employee—to introduce the new employee to co-workers, provide them with office supplies, and offer insights about the company's culture. Sponsors devote 30 minutes a day to their charges for the duration of the two-week orientation period.

———

Every month, Bread Loaf Construction Company in Middlebury, Vermont, picks an employee from the field to be given a complete tour of the company's offices and construction sites. This gives employees a better sense of what other workers in the company do and it helps them to establish links with office and administrative employees.

———

At pawnshop chain Cash America Investments, based in Fort Worth, Texas, all employees—from secretaries all the way up to the president—spend time working in a store to learn how to appraise goods and write loans.

> **"The conclusions are unambiguous. Companies that invest in their workers and give their workers greater responsibility do far better than their competitors."**
>
> ROBERT REICH
> Former U.S. Secretary of Labor

> 66 The need to pay more attention to quality and productivity is another reason for front-line workers' increased involvement in production decisions. Flexible, highly skilled employees can provide better service than do workers who can offer only narrow specialized service. 99
>
> RAY MARSHALL
> Former U.S. Secretary
> of Labor

When a store clerk calls the home office for advice, employees can provide assistance based on their experience.

Jim Baka, president of CERAC, a specialty chemical maker in Milwaukee, Wisconsin, cross-trains employees to ensure that they understand how their work fits into the overall operation. According to Baka, the results speak for themselves: "Thanks to cross-training, we've been able to push sales up 15 to 20 percent per year, while maintaining a high-quality product, delivering performance, and providing technical customer assistance."

When managers at Quad/Graphics, based in Pewaukee, Wisconsin, gather for an annual two-day conference, they leave nonmanagement personnel in charge of operations. According to an employee, "You've got to trust everybody you're working with to get things done."

Sunnyvale, California, computer maker Amdahl teamed up with a local junior college to offer the company's non-college-graduates a chance to get a degree. The program offers courses in quality assurance, inventory control, management principles, and accounting, all taught at Amdahl. Employees can attend for up to five hours a week on company time and Amdahl picks up the tab for textbooks.

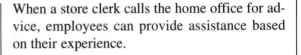

At Los Angeles-based Accountants Overload, a firm that specializes in the placement of accounting, bookkeeping, and data entry professionals on a temporary and full-time basis, every employee has the opportunity to participate in a Chairman's Special Project—helping to fulfill the company's vision and learning to become a leader in the process. For example, Accounts Overload manager of training and development, Dianna Shafai, was selected to spearhead a Chairman's Special Project that involved contacting job candidates and informing them about the company's bonus referral program through which employees are rewarded for referring new hires to the company. She promoted the program and generated many new referrals at the same time.

> 66Companies that don't encourage employee education of all kinds are dumb.99
>
> TOM PETERS
> Management Consultant

At Lowe's Companies, the second-largest U.S. building supply retailer, headquartered in North Wilkesboro, North Carolina, all vice presidents and managers are required to work in one of the retail stores for a week. Not only does this give managers a better appreciation for what life is like on the frontline of the business, but it gives headquarters staff the chance to get to know regular employees—making the organization a better place to work for managers and workers alike.

Automobile manufacturer Honda of America in Marysville, Ohio, is a big believer in employee development as a way to upgrade the

A Climate of Trust

According to *Training & Development* magazine, empowering employees requires leaders to create a climate in which employees know that:

1. They are integral to the organization and can improve it.

2. Good ideas will be implemented.

3. Suggestions that are not accepted will still be appreciated and rewarded by management.

4. They can be trusted with responsibility.

5. They are respected for their ideas and judgment.

skills of employees while improving their morale and involvement. Honda's training facility offers more than 300 classes, including engineering, English, and Japanese—most taught by Honda employees. Most production associates spend about a week in the classroom each year. Selected workers are sent to Japan for specialized training in team leadership and production methods.

———

Viking Freight System in San Jose, California, uses a formal mentoring program to help nonmanagement employees move into management jobs. In a recent year, more than two-thirds of the mentored were promoted. Viking's mentoring program energizes both the mentors and students who participate.

———

Over the course of a year, Phelps County Bank of Rolla, Missouri, conducted an in-house training program to educate staffers about all the aspects of the bank. Each department prepared an hour-long presentation about its functions for the rest of the organization. After all the departments had made their presentations, staff played a simulated game of "Jeopardy," complete with an electric scoreboard, to test their knowledge.

———

As part of its process improvement training program, the Michigan Department of Transportation issues a "license to change" to each participant. The laminated license, signed by the agency head and deputy director of quality, expresses management's support of employee efforts to break out of their day-to-day routines to improve processes and quality.

———

Instead of laying off employees when markets for certain products decline, Motorola in Schaumburg, Illinois, has a policy of retraining them. This commitment has led to the development of one of the most extensive and successful training efforts of any corporation. It's Motorola's policy that every worker has the right to retraining and, if the worker fails the retraining, he still has a right to a job at Motorola. Eventually, a fit will be found for the employee.

———

Management at Honda of America, located in Marysville, Ohio, creates energizing opportunities for its employees by assigning them high-risk, high-reward projects. For example, those employees assigned to new model development make trips to Japan, are exposed to new technology, work under short timelines, and are afforded lots of visibility. Says John Ball, manager of service training, "So when you pull off a successful new model segment, you're a hero!"

———

Garden City, New Jersey, car rental giant Avis— which is 100 percent employee owned— makes it a point to promote employees from within. Entry-level management jobs are posted

> **"I'm a strong believer in the philosophy of 'The more employees know, the more valuable they are to the company.'"**
>
> GAIL HERING
> CEO, Atmospherer
> Processing Inc.

> 66Powerlessness corrupts. Absolute powerlessness corrupts absolutely.99
>
> ROSABETH MOSS KANTER
> Professor,
> Harvard Business School

nationwide through an electronic mail system to all of Avis's field offices. According to human resources representative, Carol Riley, "If there is a shift manager job open in Atlanta, and a rental sales agent in Omaha is interested in it, he or she can apply for the position."

———

Employers who are supportive of employee attempts to better themselves—even if it means that they lose good workers—energize their workforce by demonstrating that their first concern is the overall welfare of the employees. Management at Novartis (formerly Sandoz Pharmaceuticals Corporation) based in Basel, Switzerland, lets its employees know that it doesn't consider them disloyal for considering career paths that lead outside the company. Novartis believes that offering employees ways to enhance their future employability alleviates the anxiety connected with losing a job and demonstrates that the company truly cares about them as people.

———

Ore-Ida Foods, a unit of the H.J. Heinz Company in Pittsburgh, Pennsylvania, sponsors a fellows program in which five individuals are given control over a $50,000 budget per year for two years to invest in product development, cost reduction, or new processes.

———

Work Environment and Benefits

A n organization's overall facilities and environment can make a tremendous difference in the attitude and energy of its employees. Is the organization set up in such a way that encourages employees to work together or does it create divisions that discourage or even undermine cooperation and collaboration? Don't forget—most workers spend about a third of their lives at work. The workplace should be a comfortable, inviting place that employees can look forward to, rather than dread spending time in.

Hearing-aid maker Oticon in Copenhagen, Denmark, helped to foster employee autonomy, creativity, and customer responsiveness by removing the partitions from its administrative office cubicles and installing a computer network linking all employees. Now, all 130 corporate staffers work in one big, open room. Teams use any desks they like, changing from day to day according to the needs of the project.

The parking area of aerospace parts manufacturer Moog's circular plant in East Aurora, New York, wraps around the building so that employees see other production areas daily as they pass them on the way to their own jobs.

> ❝I don't think it's possible to make a great quality product without having a great quality work environment. So it's linked—quality product, quality customer service, quality workplace, and quality of life for your employees.❞
>
> YVON CHOUINARD
> CEO, Patagonia

> 66We try very con-
> sciously to eliminate
> any differentiation
> between manage-
> ment and everybody
> else. That's the rea-
> son we don't have
> any assigned parking
> places, no executive
> dining rooms. Every-
> body wears the same
> colored hard hat.
> Green is the color
> you wear. No gold
> hats for the
> president.99
>
> KEN IVERSON
> Chairman, Nucor Corp.

This gives them an appreciation of what other employees do and a sense of the mission of the whole organization.

To improve employee communication, Roberts Express, a trucking firm based in Akron, Ohio, completely redesigned its office space—installing low-walled cubicles in place of walled offices. The change met its goals by allowing employees to interact more easily and more often.

At San Francisco's *Wired* magazine, the large, open office includes two "living-room" meeting areas, complete with coffee tables, sofas, and a stereo system stocked with more than 200 compact discs available for employees to choose among.

At the software giant Microsoft, espresso bars are open 12 hours a day, an ultra-casual dress code is the rule, and employees are often found playing basketball or tossing around a Frisbee outside the Redmond, Washington, headquarters. Says summer intern Will Kennedy, "The environment is what persuaded me to come back to Microsoft for a second summer as an intern. Sure, I looked elsewhere, but no other company would let me wear shorts and play golf in the halls."

When Sun Microsystems, a computer work-station manufacturer, designed its new facility in Menlo Park, California, the company hired a consultant to study the natural interactions of employees in the workplace. Based on the consultant's observations, the architects designed forum spaces and sun rooms to encourage the spontaneous, but productive, conversations employees have when they encounter each other casually outside of the formal office setting.

———

A leader can set the tone for an entire organization by the energizing symbols that he or she chooses to employ. The sign outside Mary Kay Cosmetics founder Mary Kay Ash's office in Dallas reads "Department of Sunshine and Rainbows." "Such thinking permeates the whole company," says Ash. "It's genuine, and they all know that."

———

All employees at Intel, a computer micro-processor manufacturer headquartered in Sunnyvale, California, work in open cubicles rather than in traditional, closed offices. Even Andrew Grove, the president and CEO, is assigned to a cubicle. According to Grove, this policy supports the company's policy of "intellectual honesty," in which employees are encouraged to tell him and each other what they really think.

———

SUGGESTION BOX

Energize employees by improving their work environment. The following environmental factors help people feel and do their best. Their absence can be a source of stress and annoyance.

- Plants
- Framed artwork
- Clean, unworn carpets
- Adequate ventilation and light
- Plenty of meeting space
- Privacy
- Adequate workspace
- Proper and well-functioning equipment
- Pleasant reception area
- Adequate break/lunch facilities
- Fitness room

❝Our clients are the reason for our existence as a company, but to serve our clients best, we have to put our people first. People are a company's one true competitive measure.❞

HAL ROSENBLUTH
CEO, Rosenbluth
International

After revenues and the number of staffers both fell 25 percent at Chaix & Johnson, a design firm in Los Angeles, managing director Scott Kohno moved out of his office and into the middle of the work floor. Since the move, Kohno says, his staff contact "is 100 times more frequent. There are a million little discussions that move the company 10 times faster. The energy level has totally changed."

To encourage the spontaneous exchange of ideas, Procter & Gamble consumer goods marketer and manufacturer has placed couches in various locations throughout its Cincinnati headquarters building.

Because of the silence that tends to prevail in elevators, the Aluminum Company of America installed escalators in hopes of keeping conversations going when employees are on the move in its new Pittsburgh, Pennsylvania, headquarters facility.

Kyoto, Japan-based industrial equipment manufacturer Omron Corporation equipped one of its factories with waist-high conveyor belts and height-adjustable work stations, to accommodate employees using wheelchairs.

The Stride Rite Corporation, maker of children's shoes, headquartered in Cambridge,

Massachusetts, offers subsidized on-site child care *and* adult care facilities. Their commitment to employees is so firm that Stride Rite's management insisted that a new venture partner in Thailand open a day care center for its employees, too.

———

Prospect Associates, a health research and communications company based in Rockville, Maryland, allows its employees to bring their children to work as long as they are well behaved and do not disturb operations.

———

Newton, North Carolina, manufacturer Ridgeview Hosiery arranges for school counselors to meet on-site with parents during regular working hours. Not only are employees convenienced by not having to leave the plant for meetings, the company suffers less from disruption of its schedule.

———

First Interstate Bank of California in Los Angeles offers free pagers to its employees so spouses can keep in touch with them during the last months of a woman's pregnancy.

———

To encourage wellness in its large number of employees whose jobs involve travel, the Union Pacific Railroad established Project Health Track. In the first phase of the program, the Omaha, Nebraska-based railroad established contracts with more than 100 private

> **"From an employee standpoint, a great place to work is one in which you trust the people you work for, take pride in what you do, and enjoy the people you are working with."**
>
> ROBERT LEVERING
> *A Great Place to Work*

Energy Points

In his newsletter *Fast Forward*, management consultant Tom Peters offers the following advice for creating an energized workplace:

■ Do excellent work, known around the world for its innovativeness.

■ Attract exciting people — more than a few of whom are a little offbeat.

■ Raise hell, question "the way things are done around here," and never, ever rest on your laurels. (Today's laurels are tomorrow's compost.)

■ Make sure those who leave, voluntarily or involuntarily, testify as to having learned a lot, had a special experience, and made fast friends while they were here. (Ye shall be known by your alumni!)

■ Create a collegial, supportive, zany, laughter-filled environment where folks support one another and office "politics" are as absent as is possible in a human (i.e. imperfect) enterprise.

■ Never allow a question or innuendo to surface about your ethics.

Continued on opposite page.

gyms in 20 states, allowing employees to work out whenever they are on the road. In the second phase, they converted seven railroad cars into traveling mini-gyms. These rolling gyms follow railroad workers wherever they go— regardless of how remote the location. Since the program was introduced two years ago, health claims from non-chronic conditions have been cut in half.

———

Jack Stack, President and CEO of SRC Corporation, an engine rebuilding company in Springfield, Missouri, established a recreation committee at each of the company's plants. The eight employees, elected each year, are provided with a $5,000 budget to fund recreational and sports activities.

———

Brinker International, a Dallas-based restaurant group, sponsors regular indoor miniature golf tournaments at its headquarters building. The switchboard is shut down, employees dress up for the occasion, and all present participate in a rousing nine-hole game of golf.

———

When Gary Comer, founder of Lands' End, the Dodgeville, Wisconsin-based mail-order house, built an 80,000 square-foot activity center as a *$9 million* gift to his employees, he asked them to submit their ideas about what facilities the center should include. The completed center houses a 25-meter swimming pool (high on the employee wish lists), a glass-walled indoor track, an exercise equipment room, a whirlpool, a gymnasium, a photographic dark-room, and outdoor tennis courts and picnic areas. At one end of the pool, 1,300 employees hand-lettered their names on the tiles. Comer's dedication reads, "These are the names of the people whose daily work and good spirit at Lands' End have made this building possible. It is dedicated to them and to their continued good health."

Cleveland computer-services firm JasTech gives its employees the option of choosing between two different benefit programs. The first choice is a standard package of company-selected benefits. The second choice is a "cafe-teria plan" that allows employees to pick and choose their own benefits and pocket any savings as pay.

At Vancouver City Savings Credit Union in British Columbia, management has implemented Living Well, an employee wellness program designed to encourage positive behavior and healthy living. Adapted from the organization's old fitness program, Living Well encourages employees to spend time with their families, and offers seminars on topics such as safety, physical activity, education, and financial planning.

- Dot the i's, cross the t's, answer the phones promptly, send out errorless invoices, and, in general, never forget that "the devil is in the details."

- Work with exciting customers (and other partners) who turn you on, who stretch you, from whom you can learn, and who are fun to be around (and who pay their bills on time, too!).

- Take in substantially more money than you spend (but make sure spending includes above-average compensation and a very high level of investment in the future).

- Grow via quality ser-vices and customers, not mere growth for growth's sake.

A "People Objective"

Dallas-based plumbing and air conditioning installer TDIndustries has developed the following "people objective":

"Each and every TD person should feel successful as a person —with his co-workers, his family, his friends, his community, his God, and himself. Among other things, this means he must feel growth, must feel individually important—and it requires of him a high order of responsibility and self-discipline. If through oversight, neglect, or just not caring much, we fail to do what we can to help even one person in this objective, it's really a bad failure. For this concept to be real, it must be total. There must be no one excluded."

The Illinois Trade Association in Glenview reimburses its employees for chiropractic, herbal therapy, and other nontraditional medical treatments. In addition, once a month every employee is eligible to receive a free massage on company time. The organization hasn't lost a single employee in five years.

———

To help employees pay for their health insurance, restaurant owner George MacLeod of Bucksport, Maine, allows his employees to split the restaurant's profits one Sunday a month. Participating employees have made enough money to cover the entire cost of their health insurance premiums.

———

Redwood City, California-based VeriFone has implemented the VeriGift program, through which employees can donate unneeded vacation time to a "vacation bank." The time is distributed to employees of the credit-card transaction systems manufacturer who are experiencing personal hardships and have exhausted their own leave.

———

Media power Bloomberg in New York City has a food court—stocked with coffee, soda, fresh fruit, and candy bars—in the middle of its reception area. This updated version of the old water-cooler energizes employees and facilitates the sharing of information.

———

The Longaberger Company, a producer of handcrafted items in Dresden, Ohio, has an on-site clinic with an around-the-clock nurse and a doctor on call every weekday to provide free medical care to employees and family members.

———

Employees have been known to show their appreciation for having an employer that cares about them. To mark the 100th birthday of Racine, Wisconsin's, S.C. Johnson Wax, a manufacturer of household products, *95 percent* of the employees in the Racine area made personal contributions—averaging $125 each—toward replacing the globe mounted in front of the headquarters building. The effort, known as Project Mum, was a complete surprise to CEO Samuel C. Johnson, who was on a business trip when the new, carbon-fiber globe was installed. Needless to say, he was pleased when his employees presented him with their gift.

———

To help associates better balance their careers and their personal lives, Marriott International, a global leader in the hospitality industry, based in Bethesda, Maryland, established a Work-Life Programs department. To accomplish its mission, the department established a child development center; child-care discounts; family-care spending accounts; referral services for child, elder, and family care issues; and many other innovative and energizing programs. Because of programs such as these, Marriott has been named one of the 100 Best Companies for Working Mothers by *Working Mother* magazine.

> **"**By providing part-timers with insurance, we've helped bring turnover to less than 50 percent in an industry where it typically runs more than 100 percent annually. Thanks to lower turnover, we've saved more in training costs than we've spent on insurance.**"**
>
> HOWARD SCHULTZ
> CEO, Starbucks Coffee Company

Employee Ownership and Stock Options

Approximately 9,500 American companies—representing about 10 percent of the country's workforce—have employee stock-ownership plans. Employees who own a part of the company they work for and who have a say in how it is run—whether through stock ownership, or other vehicles—are much more likely to work for the company's financial health in whatever way they can than employees who only have a paycheck to show for their efforts. According to a recent study, employee-owned firms "significantly outperformed their competitors in both employment growth and sales growth." On average, the growth rate of companies that have employee stock ownership plans (ESOPs) and engage in participative management programs is three to four times greater than that of those that don't. Many employers now realize that their employees need more than an hourly paycheck to energize them and involve them in the organization—they need ownership.

Employees at Wal-Mart, headquartered in Bentonville, Arkansas, are known internally as *associates* and managers are called *coaches* instead of supervisors, managers, or bosses. All are shareholders in the company. As owners, they receive regular financial performance reports. As a result, Wal-Mart has become one of the most successful major retailers in the country.

> **"Treat employees like partners, and they act like partners."**
>
> —FRED ALLEN
> Chairman,
> Pitney Bowes Co.

A cipco (American Cast Iron Pipe Company), which operates the world's largest iron foundry at its plant in Birmingham, Alabama, has a long history of encouraging a sense of ownership in its employees. In addition to a base pay scale that is in the top 25 percent of similar facilities, Acipco pays its employees quarterly dividends based on the company's profitability. Says design engineer Mike Kitchens, "Most people treat the job as if they're spending their own money." Employees own the company and exert control over its direction by serving on its board of directors, which is comprised of top managers and four elected non-management employees. According to Cynthia Lovoy, Acipco's publicity manager, this arrangement was created by the company's founder so that "the workers and the management should communicate with each other, be able to sit down and listen to each other."

———

A t engine rebuilder SRC Corporation in Springfield, Missouri, employees own the company. One way that SRC involves its employee/owners in decision making is through the use of what is known as the "Great Game of Business"—the company's unique form of open-book management. Introduced by President and CEO Jack Stack, the Great Game teaches all employees how to understand the company's financial data. They are then invited to monitor weekly income statements and cash-flow reports, and to compare actual results against projected results. Employees receive

SUGGESTION BOX

If you can't give your employees a financial stake in your business, the next best thing is to provide a sense of ownership. Here are a few ways to create a sense of pride and belonging among employees:

☛ *Make sure employees know what the organization stands for, its purpose, values, and who it serves.*

☛ *Let people know how they and their jobs fit into the larger organization and how they fit into the organization's goals.*

☛ *Give everyone business cards even if they don't deal with customers or vendors.*

☛ *Encourage employees to contribute their ideas and, if possible, let them develop the idea to its fruition.*

> **❝**It takes people 18 months to 'get' how we work here. We have to teach the concept of ownership. We tell people, 'This is *your* company.' That's a new idea to most people. School teaches you to obey authority. We teach people to think for themselves.**❞**
>
> MAGGIE HUGHES
> President, LifeUSA

quarterly bonuses based on selected financial goals such as return on assets. According to Stack, "What they learn is how to make money, how to make a profit. The more people understand, the more they want to see the result."

———

Southwest Airlines, headquartered in Dallas, developed the first profit-sharing program in airline industry. Southwest requires that all employees invest at least a quarter of their profit-sharing funds in company stock. Employees are provided with regular financial and performance data so they can monitor the effectiveness of the operation. As a result, Southwest has won the industry's "triple crown"—fewest lost bags, fewest complaints, best on-time performance— a record eight times. In fact, Southwest is the *only* airline to have won the triple crown.

———

In the utilities building at the Allied Signal Industrial Fibers plant in Moncure, North Carolina, every piece of large equipment—including huge steam boilers, air compressors, and more—is assigned an employee "owner." Ownership is acknowledged by large signs attached to each machine that spell out in large letters *"This steam boiler owned by . . ."* an employee's name added. According to Jim Middleton, a manager at the plant, "Not only does this ensure that the equipment is maintained properly, but it is a great source of pride to our employees."

———

CASE STUDY:
SOMETHING'S BREWING AT STARBUCKS

To say that Starbucks Coffee has taken the country by storm is an understatement. It seems that anywhere you go today—whether you're downtown, in the suburbs, or even at the airport—a new Starbucks store has appeared, and is selling its premium coffees and coffee accessories to a populace eager to partake. The Seattle-based company has more than 400 retail stores and 26 major airport locations, as well as a thriving mail-order business and direct sales to businesses such as Nordstrom, Barnes & Noble bookstores, and the Delta shuttle. All told, more than two million people drink Starbucks coffee each week.

Employees Come First

How has Starbucks become such a success? Certainly, the high quality of their products, the ambiance of the stores, and the current trendiness of sipping steaming cappuccinos or *mocha grandes* have played a large part. However, of at least equal importance are Starbucks employees. And critical to this element is the way that Starbucks involves its employees in the business of making and selling coffee.

The company articulates its commitment to its employees in the first point of its mission statement:

> ...establish Starbucks as the premier purveyor of the finest coffee in the world while maintaining our uncompromising principles as we grow. The following five guiding principles will help us measure the appropriateness of our decisions:
>
> 1. Provide a great work environment and treat each other with respect and dignity.
>
> 2. Apply the highest standards of excellence to the purchasing, roasting, and fresh delivery of our coffee.
>
> 3. Develop enthusiastically satisfied customers all of the time.
>
> 4. Contribute positively to our communities and to our environment.
>
> 5. Recognize that profitability is essential to our future success.

The company is a model of employee ownership, involvement, and communication. The result is a superior product, coupled with customer service. The icing on the cake is

Continued on next page.

sales growth of 65 percent a year over the last three years while net income skyrockets by 70 to 100 percent a year.

All Starbucks employees—known internally as "partners"—start their careers with 24 hours of classroom training at one of the company's regional training centers. New hires learn about a wide variety of topics, including retail skills, coffee brewing methods, customer service, and pouring the "perfect" shot of espresso (in 18 to 23 seconds). The courses are taught by district managers, specialists, and training managers who know the subjects *and* have worked in a retail store for at least two months. Managers have an additional eight weeks of classes to choose from, including "Coffee Knowledge 101" and workshops on conducting performance appraisals, recruiting, and project management.

> Starbucks was the first private company to offer stock options to both full-time and part-time employees.

The "Bean Stock" Plan

From the time he purchased the company in 1987, CEO Howard Schultz planned to institute an employee ownership program. In 1990, an internal development team took on the task of creating a stock-option plan that would not only involve partners more deeply in the company, but would give them a real stake in it. In 1991, the company implemented the "Bean Stock" plan which allows partners who are employed a minimum of six months, and who work at least 20 hours a week, to be eligible for stock options. The amount awarded to individual partners depends on several factors, including their salaries, the grant price of the stock, and the profitability of the company. With the implementation of the Bean Stock plan, Starbucks became the first private company to offer stock options to both full-time *and* part-time employees.

To keep employees informed, senior management conducts quarterly open forums in each of the company's sales regions. A broad range of issues is discussed, including expansion plans, financial information, and environmental issues, and partners are encouraged to share their ideas and suggestions with senior management. In addition to these quarterly meetings, Starbucks distributes annual Bean Stock reports to all partners, and the company publishes *Pinnacle*, a newsletter that spotlights company performance as well as the activities of individual partners company-wide. Starbucks is also using video and teleconferencing technology to reach out to its partners.

In an effort to increase employee involvement, Starbucks has instituted self-managed work teams at its roasting plants. Although plant managers and supervisors are responsible for the initial organization of the teams, partners are encouraged to take over day-to-day operations, including decision making. Cross-functional teams of partners and supervisors make hiring decisions together. Everyone on the team has a voice in the process, and partners are encouraged to offer their views on the candidate's potential compatibility with the company. The company's "Mission Review Team"—comprised of partners from throughout the company—visits Starbucks outlets to check the consistency of their operations and make sure they adhere to the company's guiding principles.

Benefits for All

Employee benefits are another company strength, one that helps to keep employee turnover at approximately 65 percent—far less than the industry average of 150 to 400 percent. In 1987, Starbucks decided to give all employees—including part-time partners—full health-care benefits. If a partner works at least 20 hours a week, he or she is eligible to receive benefits after only 90 days on the job. The health plan—which pays 90 to 100 percent of medical costs with a $10 co-payment—costs employees less than $400 a year. Dental insurance and optical care are provided for free. Disability and life insurance are also included in the benefits package.

Partners are invited to join the company's 401(k) retirement plan after serving one year. The company contributes 25 cents for every dollar the employee puts in. It also provides vacation time, two personal days off each year, price discounts on Starbucks merchandise, and a free pound of coffee every week. All employees have access to a benefits "Help Line" which partners can call to ask questions about their stock or other benefits. The company also offers an employee assistance program, dependent-care reimbursement accounts, and an employee recognition program.

All in all, Starbucks offers a diverse range of opportunities and benefits to its partners. It's little wonder that three to five new stores continue to open every week, and that employees are making their careers at Starbucks.

UTC Tips

Hartford, Connecticut-based diversified manufacturer United Technologies Corporation gives its supervisors these guidelines for empowering others:

■ Create a keen sense of ownership in those who do the work.

■ Encourage others to initiate tasks or projects they think are important.

■ Act as a "coach" as opposed to a "player" when working with staffers.

■ Share your power in the interest of the overall organizational goal.

■ Encourage others to take responsibility even when it has not been clearly assigned.

■ Assist others in uncovering new opportunities, even if they cannot all be pursued.

■ Reward others for innovation and calculated risk taking.

■ Delegate responsibility to the lowest level that can handle the task.

At LifeUSA, an insurance company located in Minneapolis, Minnesota, there are no employees—only owners. The reason? Robert W. MacDonald, founder of the company and former president of ITT Life, says, "People should not be treated the way corporations often treat them. It isn't right, and it isn't efficient." The owners of LifeUSA—all of whom receive approximately 10 percent of their compensation in the form of stock options—are more efficient and more effective than the employees of similar firms. According to MacDonald, "We write more business than probably 98 percent of the companies out there. And we do it with fewer people. Because they're owners, they're involved, they run the company." Employees control options on more than 1.8 million shares of stock, or approximately 4,500 for each employee. To help them learn how they can contribute to improving the value of their stock, LifeUSA conducts quarterly financial briefings for employees called "Share the Wealth" meetings, and senior staffers teach classes in marketing, customer service, and other business topics.

———

National Telephone & Communications in Irvine, California, which more than tripled its revenue in one year—to $31 million—finds that *nothing* energizes employees like owning a piece of the company. *Every* employee receives stock options (200 shares minimum) that even at the lowest levels is equal to a year's salary.

———

After Avis, the car rental company headquartered in Garden City, New Jersey, became an employee-owned company, its complaint rate dropped 35 percent and its stock value rocketed 400 percent in two years.

———

At Lowe's, the national lumber store chain, headquartered in North Wilkesboro, North Carolina, employees own 25 percent of the company. Each store elects a representative to an advisory committee that hears management reports and makes recommendations, and each store holds a monthly meeting for employees to discuss changes in operating procedures and merchandising. As a result, productivity at Lowe's is 200 to 300 percent above industry average and employee theft is less than one-sixth the normal rate.

———

66Owners, real owners, don't have to be told what to do—they can figure it out for themselves. They have all the knowledge, understanding, and information they need to make a decision, and they have the motivation and the will to act fast.99

JACK STACK
President and CEO,
SRC Corporation

Community Involvement

These days, the best organizations are involved in and contribute to their communities. While the number of ways companies can get involved is endless, it all boils down to helping find ways to make their communities better places to live, work, and do business through the sharing of resources, the labor of their employees, or just plain old-fashioned cash.

One of the best ways for an organization to get involved in its community is to tap the energy of its employees. Maryland spice manufacturer McCormick and Company opens its plants one Saturday each year for "Charity Day," a day when employees voluntarily work their normal shifts for no pay. In return for their volunteering, McCormick donates twice the employee's daily wage to the charity of his or her choice. On a recent Charity Day, $769,000 was raised for local charity groups. Efforts like these energize employees by involving them in projects they know are valuable to their community.

> **"We lead by being human. We do not lead by being corporate, professional or institutional."**
>
> PAUL HAWKEN, Founder, Smith & Hawken

NationsBank in Charlotte, North Carolina, encourages all of its employees to spend up to two paid hours per week helping in community schools. Employees are energized by the opportunity to do community service on company time.

Employees at the Little Hampton, England-based personal care products company the Body Shop are required to spend one hour per week of company time on a public-service project.

—

Computer Media Technology, a manufacturer of recordable media for computers based in Sunnyvale, California, encourages its employees to volunteer for community service projects during working hours. The company posts a list of local organizations such as soup kitchens or homes for the elderly that need help. Says owner Clay Teramo, "Volunteering helps keep work from becoming a grind."

—

A committee of Xerox employees reviews requests by their peers to participate in the company's social service leave program. Some 400 employees of the Stamford, Connecticut-based company have taken from a month to a year off with pay to pursue socially responsible projects, including caring for AIDS patients, providing legal aid for the poor, and counseling drug addicts. Xerox also has a program that gives grants to employees to make improvements in their communities. Projects funded have included cleaning parks, tutoring disadvantaged children, and running a health awareness workshop.

—

Some 8,600 employees of the San Francisco-based Bank of America pledged to protect

SUGGESTION BOX

☞ Give employees the opportunity to support their beliefs on company time.

☞ Let employees vote on which charities will receive corporate gifts.

☞ Make your organization a positive force in your community.

> ❝Look at a well-run company and you will see the needs of its stockholders, its employees, and the community at large being served simultaneously.❞
>
> ARNOLD HIATT,
> Former CEO,
> Stride Rite Corp.

the environment while on the job. The employees established an Environmental Awareness Day, expanded company recycling efforts, and volunteered for local cleanup projects.

———

Instead of hitting the golf course, attendees at the Skyline Displays annual sales meeting in Burnsville, Minnesota, pitched in to build a playground for area children. The cost for the portable tradeshow displays company—four days of work and $60,000—was about the same as the annual trek to a golf resort.

———

A sign above the reception desk at Salem Sportswear in Hudson, New Hampshire, reads "No ties beyond this point." Anyone caught wearing a tie, including visitors, is fined $2, with the proceeds going to charity.

———

Employees at Beckman Instruments, a scientific instrument manufacturer in Fullerton, California, take turns organizing "Beckman Volunteers"—groups that do fund-raising walkathons to support a variety of research-related, nonprofit organizations.

———

Ben & Jerry's Homemade of Waterbury, Vermont, sets aside 1 percent of its profits to be donated to programs that promote peace.

———

Employees at Tandem Computers in Cupertino, California, can apply for public service sabbaticals that include not only paid time away from the office, but financial support for the projects the employees engage in. Projects have included a study of nutrition in Zimbabwe, teaching English to young people in Poland, and road building in Tanzania.

———

Atlanta-based United Parcel Service spends $10,000 for each manager it sends through the company's community internship program. The 30-year-old program sends managers to a non-profit community service agency for a month to work with the agency's staff and clients. A typical day might include painting a building, serving meals to the homeless, or talking with program directors at soup kitchens or drug rehabilitation centers. More than 1,000 managers have participated in the program.

———

When Hurricane Andrew hit the Miami area in 1992, the *Miami Herald* and its corporate parent, Knight-Ridder, went out of their way to help employees whose lives were devastated by the storm. The companies rented out a block of hotel rooms to house employees and their families who had lost their homes; granted immediate $5,000 signature loans to employees who requested them; and distributed huge amounts of food, water, and other supplies donated by Knight-Ridder employees throughout the country. A

High-Performance Characteristics

In its report, *The Road to High-Performance Workplaces: A Guide to Better Jobs and Better Business Results,* the Department of Labor's Office of the American Workplace identified the following characteristics of high-performance organizations:

1. Opportunity for training and continuous learning.

2. Sharing of information.

3. Employee participation.

4. Flat organizational structures.

5. Cross-level employee partnerships.

6. Compensation linked to performance.

7. Layoffs avoided at all cost.

8. Supportive work environment.

9. Integration of all of these practices into the organization's long-term strategy.

> **"**Ironically, the projects that begin small and with cultural goals often generate greater proportional financial returns than those with economic goals.**"**
>
> ROSABETH MOSS KANTER
> *When Giants Learn*
> *to Dance*

group of 50 employees of the *Miami Herald* wrote: "During the recent events, Knight-Ridder and the *Miami Herald* have displayed an incredible degree of caring that could never be found in an institution that *only* cares for its 'bottom line'. . . . We feel privileged to work for a company like OURS."

———

Fairfield Inn by Marriott, a division of Marriott International, a global hospitality provider based in Bethesda, Maryland, has established a formal partnership with Habitat for Humanity International to help build simple, decent homes for qualifying low-income families. Fairfield Inn employees actively participate in the program by volunteering their labor to help build the homes and by assisting in fund-raising efforts.

———

Silver Dollar City, an 1880s Ozark village theme park in Branson, Missouri, sets aside a pool of money to provide financial assistance to employees who are struggling. The assistance is given with no payback schedule. While most recipients eventually pay back the money, it is not required that they do so.

———

Richer Sounds, the United Kingdom's largest stereo equipment dealer, sets aside 1 percent of its profits in an employee hardship fund. The fund provides grants and interest-free loans to employees who suffer unforeseen or catastrophic financial hardship.

———

Index

ABOUT BOB NELSON

BOB NELSON is founder of Nelson Motivation, Inc., and a vice president of Blanchard Training and Development in San Diego. He is the author of 17 books on business and management, including *1001 Ways to Reward Employees, Consulting For Dummies, Motivating Today's Employees, Managing For Dummies,* and *Empowering Employees Through Delegation,* as well as *365 Ways to Manage Better Page-A-Day® Perpetual.* He holds an MBA from the University of California at Berkeley and is a doctoral candidate in the Executive Management Program of The Peter F. Drucker Graduate Management Center of The Claremont Graduate School in Los Angeles. He lives in San Diego.

Mr. Nelson is publisher of a monthly newsletter, *Rewarding Employees,* and has created a variety of additional products including videos, audios, software, learning tools and more to help put concepts from his books into practice. For information about his newsletter and available products or to schedule Mr. Nelson or one of his associates to consult or present to your company, association, or conference, contact:

1-800-575-5521
Nelson Motivation, Inc.
P.O. Box 500872
San Diego, CA 92150-9973
619-673-0690/619-673-9031 (fax)
E-mail: BobRewards@aol.com
Website: www.nelson-motivation.com

COMMENTS/CORRECTIONS/ADDITIONS

This book is updated each printing. If you have any comments, corrections or additions—please send them to the address below:

Energizing Employees
P.O. Box 500872
San Diego, CA 92150-9973

If you know of an exceptional way to energize employees or have a suggestion or story that you'd like included in a subsequent edition of this book, please forward it with contact information to the above address.